More Imaginative Than Ordinary Speech

Books by Cat Ellington

REVIEWS BY CAT ELLINGTON: THE COMPLETE
ANTHOLOGY, VOL. 1

REVIEWS BY CAT ELLINGTON: THE COMPLETE
ANTHOLOGY, VOL. 2

THE MAKING OF DUAL MANIA: FILMMAKING
CHICAGO STYLE

REVIEWS BY CAT ELLINGTON - THE COMPLETE
ANTHOLOGY LIMITED EDITION HOLIDAY GIFT
SET (BOOKS 1 & 2)

REVIEWS BY CAT ELLINGTON: THE COMPLETE
ANTHOLOGY, VOL. 3

MORE IMAGINATIVE THAN ORDINARY SPEECH:
THE POETRY OF CAT ELLINGTON

More Imaginative Than Ordinary Speech

Speech

The Poetry of Cat Ellington

Cat Ellington

Quill Pen Ink Publishing

THE BEAUTY OF EXPRESSION™

CHICAGO

PAPERBACK ISBN-10: 1733442111
PAPERBACK ISBN-13: 978-1-7334421-1-4
HARDCOVER ISBN: 978-1-7370971-8-1

Library of Congress Control Number: 2022362736

Cover design: Tommie Mondell for Quill Pen Ink Publishing
Cover tint: Purple Pleasure
Flower art: Watercolors by Ateli

Published by Quill Pen Ink Publishing
Chicago, Illinois, USA
https://quill-pen-ink-publishing.business.site/

Quill Pen Ink Publishing, 2019
The Original Poetry Synopsis
The Cat Ellington Poetry Collection
The Cat Ellington Literary Collection

Watercolors by Ateli appear courtesy of Quill Pen Ink
Publishing

"The Black Girl" appears courtesy of The Black Jaguar
Music Company

Hardcover Edition: November 2021

Printed in the U.S.A.

Dedication

To Frank "Tony" McBride—
For assisting in the saving of my life all those years
ago

I will love you always

Preface

Dearest reader,

I cannot begin to tell you how thrilled I am for the release of *More Imaginative Than Ordinary Speech: The Poetry of Cat Ellington*. After receiving the first vision to write this work in 2004, I knew that I would end up having to pull it all together bit by bit over time. And although completing this work had been a challenge—due to my other professional obligations—it is finally finished. It's here now. And I couldn't be more relieved. It wasn't long after the initial vision to create this work was shown that I immediately prepared my research to study poetry book concepts. And while brainstorming ideas for titles—which, if you know me, had to be something uniquely creative—I looked up the word, *Poetry*, in my Webster's Dictionary, and voilá! There it was in the second definition: More imaginative than ordinary speech. Right away, I selected that interesting definition/description to use for the title of the work that would soon come into being: for it had been the unique title that I needed. Added, it was not in use anywhere else. And that made it all the more appealing. Indeed, it was wholly original. And it was me.

With that, I quickly jotted the words down in my notebook and allowed them to settle for a minute. And after a few more days of research, it was decided that "More Imaginative Than Ordinary Speech" would be the title of my book of poetry. And to this day, it still fascinates me.

More Imaginative Than Ordinary Speech. It was perfect. And I loved it. As far as subtitles went, that was relatively easy to decide. I favored The Poetry of Cat Ellington. It would serve as the perfect complement to the distinctive main title. Also, being a writer of songs (primarily), I could appreciate the melodic flow of all the words mingling together in perfect harmony: More Imaginative Than Ordinary Speech: The Poetry of Cat Ellington.
Yes. It was me. And it felt just right.

That was back in 2004. And today—exactly 15 years later—the beautiful vision has come to pass.

More Imaginative Than Ordinary Speech, created to feature many of my selected poems, including *The Long-suffering, The Black Diamond, The Golden Goose, Hot and Humid, The Proverbial Diva*, and *The Black Girl* (a bonus from my song catalog), was a joy to write. For is a compilation of which I am very proud. And I do hope that you, my dearest reader, will enjoy viewing this book of poetry as much as I did collecting it over the years.

Happy reading.

Acknowledgments

As always, I honor my Father God, my Lord Jesus—even Christ and Him crucified—and the gloriously awesome Holy Spirit with the first fruits of my praise: for without them, I could do nothing—creative or otherwise. And I do mean that. Thank you, my precious and omnipotent Lord, for everything that you do for me on this beautiful Earth of your making.

To my husband, Joseph, and our three cherished children Nathaniel, Nairobi, and Naras, I extend my sincerest gratitude. I love all four of you with all I have. And it pleases me to say that you're all mine.

Thank you to my beloved brothers, Freddie and Maurice, for all of your love, support, good times, good drinks, and good eats. I love you both.

Thank you to my Humanmade family. I love and appreciate all of you. Thank you for being there.

Thank you to my family of fellows at the Academy of American Poets. I love and appreciate all of you. And I thank you for your kind words.

Joanne at WorldCat, thank you, my dearest lady. I truly admire all of the hard work you do for the World's Largest Library Catalog.

Thank you, team HometownReads, for everything you all do on behalf of local authors across the country. Speaking for all of us, I can say that we appreciate every one of you.

Thank you, Gary Martin. I have loved you since we were kids in junior high, and God knows that I still love you dearly today. Thank you for your genuine friendship.

To my beloved Chad, MWAH! You still look like Rick Astley, baby, even after all these years. Haha. Thank you for just being. I love you, boo.

My dear Derek, thank you, baby. Thank you for all those times you looked out for me. I have never forgotten them, nor will I ever. I love you so much. I always have - and I always will.

For you, my dear Joyce Jackson, I have nothing but unconditional love. Thank you for always keepin' it real with me.

And to all of you, my beloved readers, I extend much love and gratitude. Thank you for absorbing my written witness with understanding.

Table of Contents

Coming November 2019: Memoirs in Gogyohka: A
Collection of Short Poems and Memoirs

About the Author

The Introduction

WHO AM I?

A Seeker of Truth.
A Finder of Truth.
A Vessel for Truth: for I am whole.

My name is Cat Ellington. And I am a woman who:

Seeks the Truth and Finds the Truth.
Gets to Know the Truth.
Falls in Love with the Truth.
Moves In with the Truth and Strives to Make Love to the Truth.
Commits Herself to the Truth and Reproduces with the Truth.
Builds A Solid Unit with the Truth and Contends with the Truth.
Sometimes Gets Frustrated with the Truth and Cries with the Truth.
Makes Amends with the Truth and Listens to the Truth.
Passes Time with the Truth.
Grows Older - and Wiser - with the Truth.
Will Die with the Truth: for the truth is what I represent. It is what I love. And it is what I choose to infuse into my creative contribution concerning the written word.

But some utterly despise the Spirit of Truth. And they hate those individuals who speak the truth boldly and who prefer to live by it. I have had run-ins with people of this sort in the past. And it is for a surety that I will continue to have run-ins with these types—whether directly or indirectly—in the present and future times. Those about whom I speak will be the ones scoffing the loudest: for they will be the proudest and the angriest. These are the people who will despise me, not so much for spotlighting the truth through the written word, but for being an African-American woman—particularly an African-American woman from the South Side of Chicago—doing it.

Know for a certainty that such hostility will stem from worldly-minded people who are full of hatred, pride, and bigotry - not to mention racism and malice. For these will be tempted to hate my being a visible public figure in the creative arts. Because my style of creativity, where it pertains to my contributions, is not overseen—much less controlled—by them or by people like them. Indeed, this is the truth.

I do me and not anyone else. And I don't - and won't - allow myself to conform to the wishes of anyone else. I write whatever the Spirit moves me, or rather, commands me to write. And if there are people out there who may be offended by my existence and my contribution to the creative arts, particularly in its branches of music, motion pictures, and literature, that's just fine; they have a right to dislike my brand. But I will not "water down" my concentrated efforts to appease anyone, nor will I sugarcoat the truth to make it more digestible to the one willing to shy away from it. That is just not going to happen. I am going to tell it like it is, and that's that. And should there be a few folks who prefer to stand in opposition to my effort(s), then so be it. But I will not don the kid gloves of conformity to appease people. It is just not in my nature. I have to be who I am. It's just that simple. Take it or leave it.

This work features poetry that took its inspiration from many of my experiences in my life. These include racism, lust, homosexuality, interracial love, rage, anger, fear, hatred, depression, manic depression, living life on the streets of the South Side of Chicago, Pentecostal Christianity, etc. Whenever there arose in my life a unique situation worthy of a written testimonial, I took the opportunity to record my witness, pen to paper. And while some of you may find my testimony inspirational, others may label the same as being quite offensive. And that's just as well with me as everything is not for everybody. But trust that my testimony is diverse and prone to mutability.

This portion of my witness I felt compelled to share through poetry. But the remainder of my witness will be reserved for my autobiography. That's right, my autobiography. Hey, if you thought the life story of Tina Turner was something, wait until you get a load of mine! Hee hee, haha.
Yes, my dearest men and women, one of these groovy ol' days, my life story will be made public via a memoir. But until then, let's start here.

I love the craft of writing because it's therapeutic, you know? There is simply no other physical gift in existence better than it. Writing is a magnificent gift that should be

cherished and nurtured but never trifled with or taken for granted.
For without the written word, nothing that has ever come into being could be or would be: for without the scribbler, what is to be of life?

The written word:
It is the beating heart of my cognitive creativity;
Its life source

It is my power.

The written word emboldens my introvert

It is my power.

The written word:
It salves the wounds of my tribulation,
It covers the scars of my despair

It is my power.

The written word:
It rebukes my persecutor - in swift defense of my honor

It is my power.

The gift of writing is one of the most special. And I am honored to be numbered among the millions of people to whom the Lord has given it.

My dearest men and women? It pleases me to present to you *More Imaginative Than Ordinary Speech: The Poetry of Cat Ellington.*

"Ignorance is not bliss, and neither is the sorrow of
the heart."
—Cat Ellington

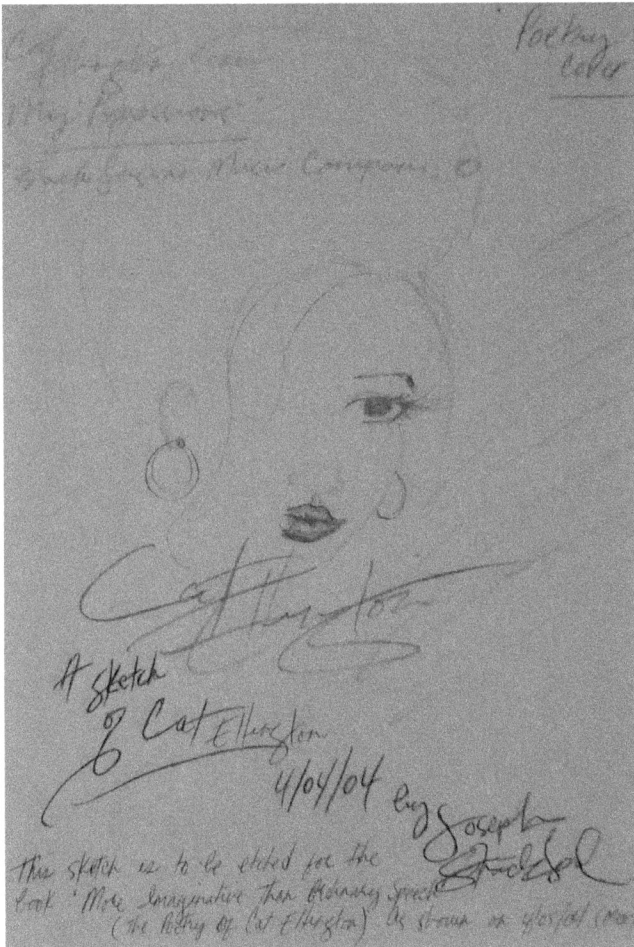

Sketch of Cat Ellington by Joseph Strickland
April 4, 2004
The beautiful vision has come to pass.

Part One

"The Beauty of Being"
Genre: Narrative

The Synopsis

This production of the written word, in poetic form, intends to praise the hated truth while rebuking the beloved lies of this present generation, which breed pride, hatred, self-hatred, low self-esteem, and idolatry – false idolatry.

The Poem:

There is beauty in peace,
There is beauty in serenity,
There is beauty in dignity,
As well as there is beauty in integrity—

There is beauty in kindness,

There is beauty in gentleness,
There is beauty in selflessness,
As well as there is in forgiveness—

There is beauty in love,
There is beauty in Heaven above,
There is beauty in the flight of a dove,
As well as there is in every preceding verse thereof—

For Man, in his very creation, is beauty:
For we are all a creation of beauty—

Regardless of race, creed, or nationality,
We are all a creation of beauty—

And every one of us is somebody.

The Poet's Commentary

There is no such person as a "nobody." Every man, and every woman, having been made by the hand of the Lord thy God, is somebody.

There is no such thing as "irrelevance" where it concerns any given human being: for the very existence of Mankind is relevant, as those of us who live play witness to that almighty power by which we've come to exist.

Weighed together, we are lighter than air. For indeed, we, as a human race, live today and are cut down tomorrow, that the Earth shall no longer provide for us a place upon its surface.

Self-love. It's a beautiful thing.

"The Longsuffering"

Genre: Narrative

The Synopsis

This production of the written word, in poetic form, intends to reflect a human spirit that remains unbroken despite oppression.

The Poem:

Despite her maniacal history,
I still love my city:

The city of Chicago...

Despite her inability to form an affinity,
I still love my city:

The city of Chicago...

Despite her second-class mentality
And her segregation of citizenry,
I still love my city:

The city of Chicago...

The city of Chicago: for she is indisputable—
Even the only city I know,
Who can have both eyes blackened
And still, be beautiful—

The city of Chicago: for she is indisputable—
Even the only city I know,
Who can have a busted lip
With a bloodied nose,
And still, be beautiful—

Despite her corruptibility,
I still love my city:

The city of Chicago...

Despite her neglect of poverty,
I still love my city:

The city of Chicago.

The Poet's Commentary

As the old saying goes, 'It's not where you live, it's how you live.' And where it regards the inspiration for *The Long-suffering*, that timeless adage is once again proven as truth.

LIKE OIL AND WATER.

In my beloved city of Chicago, where her physical beauty remains unmatched, even to this day, the spirits in many of her children—both the native and the adoptee alike—continue to spoil and rot in the scorching heat of political corruption and law-enforcement corruption - not to mention racism, street-gang violence, illegal drugs, prostitution, senseless crime, etc.

I love my city, but I do hate the godless ways of many of her children. And this would include both the Jew and the Gentile. These are my fellow Chicagoans, but many do evil. And they're tempted to do evil for sport.
Now am I banging down a gavel in judgment against any single individual? No, of course not; that's not my place. But I speak what I know. And I know my own because I come from them.

Chicago has always been a gawjus, albeit hard-nosed, town. And I love her with everything I have in me: for she is the only city in the Earth realm able to arouse so deep a love within me. And I could never be ashamed of her, nor of my having been born from the womb of her. But historically, many of her offspring have proven themselves to be quite atrocious. And in short, that had been the point of the production.

"The King of Glory"
Genre: Narrative

The Synopsis

This production of the written word, in poetic form, intends to render a testimony of one's trials and tribulations as a faithful servant of the Most-High God and the public persecutions inflicted upon him or her as a result of such faith.

The Poem:

The enemy wars against me—
Because I refuse to renounce You,
The King of Glory—

Because I refuse to renounce You,

The King of Glory,
Therefore the enemy wars against me—

For Your name,
I am—forever—defamed:
For Your name,
I bear the cross of shame—

The enemy wars against me—
Because I refuse to renounce You,
The King of Glory—

Because I refuse to renounce You,
The King of Glory,
Therefore the enemy wars against me.

The Poet's Commentary

I have said it before, and I will say it once more: I don't conform well.

REFERENCES OF TRUTH.

Truths:

"Yes, and all who desire to live godly in Christ Jesus will suffer persecution."
—II Timothy 3:12

"If the world hates you, you know that it hated me before it hated you.

If you were of the world, the world would love its own. Yet because you are not of the world, but I chose you out of the world, therefore the world hates you."
—John 15:18-19

I'm not here to preach, only to state facts so that the people may get a good understanding.

And this is understanding:

No matter who you are—Jew or Gentile, well-known or unknown, rich and wealthy or poor and needy—if you find that you're the constant target of unprovoked anger from people in the world, be they familiar persons or strangers, there is a good chance the Lord may be calling you. And the spirits in the world can detect the "light" within you.

My advice to you? Answer that spiritual phone and bid the troublers adieu.

MY (PERSONAL) TESTIMONY.

There was a time, during which I was lost in the world, that I noticed something. Wherever I went, I perceived hatred directed towards me from people out there in society. The hate towards me had not been from *everybody,* no, that would be an over-exaggeration, but there were many people. It didn't matter their race, nationality, or gender. They were just hateful towards me without just cause. Perhaps it had been my free-spirited nature? Or maybe my sense of style showcased by my wardrobe, or my height, or my hairstyles, or my cosmetic application, or my natural ability to immediately hit it off with other people whether I had known them or not, or just me being myself. Whatever the case had been, I received a lot of hate.

Such an experience isn't unique, as millions of people in the world can attest to my witness. Because they, too, are the recipients of similar treatment from both the stranger and the familiar person alike.

Being "excluded" or "alienated" from among the "crowd pleasers" was one thing when I was a young woman of the world many years ago. But on the day that I finally decided to answer that spiritual phone—which had been ringing off and on over several years—the hatred directed towards me from countless people in the world grew worse. And though it took time, I eventually learned why: the Lord was calling me. And Satan had been hatin' (through worldly people) because he knew it: the one of darkness could see the Spirit of Light on me.

WISDOM CONTINUES TO SPEAK.

"If I were of the world, the world would love its own."
—John 15:19

But there is no true love in the world, only hatred disguised as false love.

What that quote derived from the Holy Scriptures means is this. Those who are of the world are similar spiritually, and they move as a body to war against those who are not part of the evil world system. Lest anyone should seek to confuse the matter, the war-at-hand has never been physical, only spiritual. And I would rather be hated by the world for being a Pentecostal Christian woman, particularly an African-American woman of the Pentecostal faith, than a lost soul in the world system who is falsely loved (and *accepted*) by a bunch of strangers for being a practicing sinner.

Therefore, I do not receive my blessings from the hands of men but the hand of my Lord.
And His hand ain't ever short.

"A Declaration of Independence"
Genre: Free Verse

The Synopsis

This production of the written word, in poetic form, intends to witness the blessedness of independence - and of how one did not need to bow before men to receive any honor on the Earth.

The Poem:

They did not make me;
Therefore, they cannot break me—

They did not bless me;
Therefore, they cannot curse me—

They did not educate me;
Therefore, they cannot make a dummy,
They cannot make a dummy out of me—

They did not give me honor;
Therefore, they cannot disgrace me,
They cannot disgrace me with dishonor—

They did not make me;
Therefore, they cannot break me—

They did not feed me;
Therefore, they cannot starve me—

They did not clothe me;
Therefore, they cannot uncover me—

They did not give me my fame;
Therefore, they cannot take credit,
They cannot take credit for my name—

They did not make me;
Therefore, they cannot break me—

They did not make me wealthy;
Therefore, they cannot bring me to poverty—

They did not exalt me;
Therefore, they cannot humble me—

They did not make me;
Therefore, they cannot break me.

The Poet's Commentary

For it is He, the King of Kings, who has made me.
It is He, the King of Kings, who has made me—C.E.

And I render Him the praise of which He is entirely worthy.

NATURAL BORN MAVERICK.

The poetic testimony which you, my dearest reader, have just read may appear *"preachy"* enough, but it is not so much preachy as it is *"righteously indignant."*

If I must admit it, I utterly hate the idea of anyone trying to control me. Seriously, just the thought of it kindles burning anger within me. I am not keen on the idea of being swayed by other people, period. But the world in which we live is full of individuals who covet power and to have control over others, even if they must use money or their authoritative positions in society to do so.
Unfortunately, many people have weak faith. And I don't judge them because of it: some people hate to wait. Whatever the case may be, too many people have allowed themselves to fall into subjection to other human beings. And in many instances, those other human beings are in positions to control their lives.

Here is where you get the master/slave scenario:

People get told what to do and how to do it. They get told what to say and how to say it. What not to say. What to eat and what not to eat. They get told what to wear and what not to wear. Who to love and who not to love. Whose party or event to attend and whose party or event not to attend. They get told how they should look and how they should not look. They are always under scrutiny: who to appease and who not to appease - and who they should ignore. All such actions lead the one in subjection down a path of destructive anger, rage, hatred (towards themselves and others), bitterness, and self-hatred.

PUBLIC PERSECUTIONS.

Understand that those hateful men and women—under whose thumbs such people exist—are the same ones who do evil on Earth, thereby being an evil trial unto others, especially to those who find themselves in their "debt." Moreover, these same types of people despise *anyone* not under their control, pretending to ignore the targeted person but keeping a watchful eye on him or her nonetheless. And because I can't bring myself to run in the same flood of dissipation with them, therefore many are tempted to speak evil of me as a public figure.

"How come she ain't like us?" They utter among themselves.

"Who the fuck that Black bitch think she is?" They utter among themselves.

"Cat just looks like she thinks her shit don't stank." They utter among themselves.

"God, she is just so fucking narcissistic and arrogant!" They utter among themselves.

"That bitch acts like she's next to God. Ol' self-righteous ass bitch." They utter among themselves.

"I'on like no-muhhfuckin-body who thank thay betta'dan me. An'is bitch ack like she thank she betta'dan otha niggas." They utter among themselves.

"Shiiid, she got her shit, all her achievements 'n shit. But she ain't throwin' shit to no other muthafucka." They utter among themselves.

"Arrogant Black bitch!" They utter among themselves.

"Who let that nigger bitch in? Who gave her the freedom to own and operate all of those fuckin' companies in the entertainment industry? Who let that bitch in?!" They utter among themselves.

"Ain't no White-owned corporations overseeing her black ass? They ain't controlling her black ass like they control my black (or white) ass? She's just free to do what the hell she wants to do? Damn! Who allowed that? They don't own her rights 'n shit—like they own all ours?" They utter among themselves.

"If she ain't writin' shit for Bey and Cardi B and Taylor and Katy cat and Rih Rih and 'em, we don't know her." They utter among themselves.

"If she didn't get the seal of approval from Ellen, and the White people in the mainstream media don't mention her in their magazines and newspapers, she ain't important." They utter among themselves.

"She doesn't support the Kardashians and kiss their asses and validate them? Who the hell is she? Errbody else do it." They utter among themselves.

"Does she think she's better just because she's a so-called songwriter and casting director and author? Does she think she's better than the rest of us?" They utter among themselves.

"Why doesn't she support what we endorse? Why doesn't she support the LGBTQ? What's wrong with her?" They utter among themselves.

Get understanding, my dear men and women. I'm from the South Side of Chicago, even its innermost parts. And there ain't a man or a woman alive—be he or she gay or straight—who can say *anything* that's going to shock me. Neither is there even one who can out-cuss me or brandish a verbal sword bearing a double edge sharper than that of my own.

Indeed, I was living life with a bunch of hell-raising (and wig-snatchin') "dykes" and "fairies" on Chicago's South Side way before homosexuality became an *acceptable (and somewhat celebrated)* lifestyle in this here society. And I

love my men and my women. I am not ashamed of them.
No, not even one of them.

There were no *"respectable"* LGBTQ organizations back then. No one was fighting for the *"gay rights"* of my gay family members. No, my loved ones had to suffer it to be so. They were called "fags" and "bulldaggits" daily, especially on the South Side of Chicago where Black folks—in mass numbers—didn't approve of the *"alternative lifestyle"* then, and where Black folks—in mass numbers—don't approve of the *"alternative lifestyle"* now.

Back then, *"Gay pride"* didn't exist. There were no yearly *"parades"* organized either. And the only "rainbow" we knew was *Rainbow Push*—founded, of course, by the Reverend Jesse L. Jackson, Sr., respectively.

Faggot-ass muthafuckas and bulldaggit-ass bitches.

Those were some of the only words my gay relatives had ever heard spoken concerning them.

My men and my women went through the shit—way before the LGBTQ came into existence. And regardless of all the hate and persecutions they continuously endured, I, nevertheless, continued to cherish my loved ones. So do not ever falsely accuse me of fostering prejudice against anyone based on their *sexual orientation.*

Understand that I, Cat Ellington, was the original fag hag. *I* was the first person that ever used the term (in 1989), though I have never received any credit for it—being that I had only been a member of the general public during that era and not yet a public figure in the arts. Get understanding.

AS FOR THE OTHERS...

My reply to every other hateful word uttered against me is
this:

My lips don't do ass. They never have, and I don't reckon
that they soon ever will. I am who I am. Take me or leave
me.

As commanded, I will commence doing the work of my
Lord as a creative artist in the arts & entertainment industry.
And know for a certainty that not even one will be allowed
to shoo me away. Nevermind them taking offense to the hue
of my flesh and the Spirit of Truth in me.

Indeed, I come from a long line of fighters. And I intend to
stand my ground.

Trust, my dear and women, that I do not believe myself as
being better than (or as good as) anyone else. I just like my
coffee the way I like my coffee: sometimes black, sometimes
creamy, but always sweet.
I have to do things in the way I like. And not in the way that
someone else wants me to do them. Especially where it
concerns my contributions to the arts & entertainment
industry.

WISDOM. GET IT WHILE YOU CAN.

Absorb this wisdom, my dear men and women. It is the Lord
who gives one the power to get wealth. And only the Lord
can make one's name great, not people. Do not ever get it

twisted. A great name and mere fame are two different things: fame is fleeting, but a great name will stand, even until the end of time. Therefore a great name is to be desired.

Should fame seek to associate itself with anyone, there ought to be a legitimate reason why. Understand that false fame is lazy, without honor, and seeks its (own) kind with which to associate. But genuine fame—and the legitimate recognition it inevitably brings—is partial to those whose hands have toiled long and hard in his or her respective fields and crafts.

To reiterate, only the Lord God has the power to make someone's name great and to command wealth to acquaint itself with him or her, and not people. People do not have that kind of power. Only the Lord can make it possible. Only He has the power to bless people with (great) gifts, talents, and abilities. For this, His name is worthy of praise. And from my mouth, *it will be praised*.

And I thank God every day for blessing me to nurture my (creative) independence. For were it not for his blessing, I would be homeless, poverty-stricken, and hungry while waiting to be recognized - and supported - by a bunch of faithless, hateful, and self-hating people who despise both Him and me.

"The Black Diamond"

Genre: Dramatic

The Synopsis

This production of the written word, in poetic form, intends to exhibit a healthy level of self-confidence, self-esteem, and self-love short of narcissism.

The Poem:

Like a black diamond,
I shine ever so brightly.

Like a black diamond,
Brilliantly cut,
With pristine clarity—

I am a rarity—

Like a black diamond,
I shine ever so brightly.

The Poet's Commentary

She is,
She is like a black diamond:
Dark in physical hue,
Mysterious in nature,
Multifaceted in creativity,
Precious - in the vein of an uncommon jewel,
Unique,
And one of a kind.

That's me, baby.

Part Two

"The Unwavering Soul"
Genre: Dramatic

The Synopsis

This production of the written word, in poetic form, intends to proclaim one's devotion to the Lord thy God, regardless of public persecution and exclusion.

The Poem:

I will stand in my faith in Thee:
I will stand in my faith, despite the hate:
I will stand in Thee—

Despite their hate for me,
I will stand in Thee:

I will stand,
I will stand in Thee...

From my eye,
There may be many tears shed,
But I?
I will not be misled:

I will stand in Thee,
Despite their hate for me:
I will stand in Thee.

The Poet's Commentary

Here lies the conviction when one makes up his or her mind
to do it right.

The Unwavering Soul serves as the conclusion to *The King
of Glory.*

A FINAL WORD.

Stand for something lest you fall for anything, my dear men
and women.
Stand for something lest you fall for anything.

"Inspired by Imitation of Life"
Genre: Satirical

The Synopsis

This production of the written word, in poetic form, intends to witness a real-life struggle with one's racial identity, particularly within the African-American culture in modern-day society—reminiscent of the fictitious "Sara Jane Johnson."

The Poem:

I see you—to yourself being untrue:

Deceiving and being deceived,
Draggin' your manicured fingers
Through your stringy, blonde-haired weave:

I see you—to yourself being untrue:

Shameful and debased;
Fraudulently encased;
A blubbery shell of what you ate;
A pitiful embodiment of pride and self-hate:

I see you—to yourself being untrue:

In that lyin' Caste System reflection,
Passin'—with your near-White complexion:

I see you—to yourself being untrue:

Pretendin' to be one of the Caucasian persuasion,
When in fact, you know you're Black:

I see you—to yourself being untrue.

The Poet's Commentary

If there is one thing I cannot stand in life, it is self-denial,
especially when it rears its ugly head in "High Yella"
African-American people who are light-complected enough
to "pass" for White.

EXAMPLES OF SELF-RESPECT.

The late and legendary Lena Horne was fair-skinned enough to pass, but she never did. And she persevered through a much-greater hardship than those of a similar hue today.

The lovely actress, Lonette McKee, is fair-skinned enough to pass, but she never has. And she endured much worse in her time.

The beautiful actress, Jasmine Guy, is fair-skinned enough to pass, but she never has. And she had been subjected to much worse during the height of her fame.

The sexy R&B diva, Faith Evans, is fair-skinned enough to pass, but she never has, even when she could have for "mainstream acceptance."

The pretty and extremely talented Alicia Keys is fair-skinned enough to pass, but she never has, not even throughout her entire entertainment career.

And so on, and so on.

A HISTORY LESSON IN SPIRITUAL WARFARE.

Worse than self-denial (which stems from self-hatred) is cowardice (which stems from fear). Decades ago, when the world had been a different place for the oppressed in this society, namely African Americans, many light-skinned Blacks with so-called keen/European features were tempted to buckle to what was/is commonly known as the White Caste System.

A (demonic) practice enforced (and perpetuated) by human beings around the world, the Caste System serves one self-destructive purpose: to tempt people to sell their souls (or sell out) by catering to the needs and desires of Satan. This type of spiritual warfare operates through the people in the world who occupy the (ungodly) position of the oppressor, particularly those of European descent.

Satan's intention (through the evil Caste System) is to use divide-and-conquer tactics against human beings based on the flesh. Not the spirit, but the flesh. His job is to wage war against Mankind by way of the flesh. In this way, he tempts human beings to sell their souls to him in exchange for all the things in the world—based on the preferably lighter hue of their flesh. And unfortunately, countless numbers of people—the world over—have fallen for the wicked and destructive lie hook, line, and sinker: for they preferred the liar to the Spirit of Truth. And many, many generations have fallen into condemnation because of their error.

No one has ever been able to defeat spiritual forces with a carnal mind. To obtain victory in spiritual warfare, one must battle back with a spiritual-mind. It is all set in the mind. That is where the battle starts. And if oppressed people have been told—even for hundreds of years—that they are beneath someone else or the lesser, just based on the skin they were born in, those people are sure to become conditioned in their *minds*.
And Satan knows this. He knew it from the beginning, and he, the evil spirit that he is, knows it now. For he is still at war with all of Mankind. But in the country called America, he uses race. That and economics.

Because the Lord God called the oppressed people—in mass numbers—to a newfound faith in Pentecostal Christianity, it is for this reason that the devil hates and seeks to destroy people through the flesh.

One such weapon of usage in his demonic arsenal is the spirit called self-hatred. Once he can penetrate a human mind with self-hatred, he already has his war on that human won.

And whenever you see anyone—be he or she Jew or Gentile—denigrating themselves and destroying themselves to try and look like another race of people other than themselves, know for a certainty that such people are full of self-hatred.

I am not talking about hairstyling. That does not apply here. Because women, especially Black women, love to change their hair for variety. So I am not addressing various styles of hair design. I am talking about people bleaching their skins or having surgery to obtain physical attributes they were not born with: butt injections, collagen injections, rib removal (to achieve the hourglass look), cheek implants, and every other procedure of the like.

Women are paying big money, even going broke, for vanity purposes – desperate to look like someone else who they are not because of the demons called self-hatred and low self-esteem.

A Black woman will never be a White woman, and neither will a White woman ever be a Black woman. All such confusion stems from spiritual warfare - in the human mind.

Worse than a White woman pretending to act and look like a Black woman (by paying for surgical procedures to obtain those physical attributes found naturally on a Black woman) is a woman, born a very light-skinned Black, pretending to be a White woman. Such people pass for White and shamefully conduct themselves in the hope of monetary gain and acceptance in the world. And there goes self-hatred.

UNDERSTANDING IS THE NEW HEALING.

Simply telling people to love themselves and to be themselves is always easier said than done. Because the weapons of spiritual warfare have pierced too deep for far too long, and it is going to take Divine intervention to free them from their enslavement.

The fictional character by whom the production of poetry was inspired fell prey to the same spiritual forces of evil, as does the individual about whom the poem speaks.
Get wisdom. And while you are at it, grab hold of some knowledge and understanding, too.

You are who you are. And you are what you are, period. God created beauty, not ugliness. And it will be well for you to understand that you are a magnificent and unique beauty—whomever you may be.
Learn to love yourself. Learn to love yourselves.

"The Testimony of Cat Ellington"
Genre: Narrative

The Synopsis

This production of the written word, in poetic form, intends to render the author's (personal) testimony to the reader – which reveals how my past dead worldly lifestyle succumbed to a new life in Christ Jesus.

The Poem:

The queen of revelry,
Who engaged in the Trois and orgy?
Oh, how it was me:
Destitute, spiritually—

Through the looking glass of homosexuality,

I frolicked with gay empathy:
Oh, how it was me:
Destitute, spiritually—

The scoffer of marriage,
And a bosom buddy of adultery?
Oh, how it was me:
Destitute, spiritually—

Blowing my nose in the "snow,"
While diving in the sewage
Of my wickedly-frightful destiny?
Oh, how it was me:
Destitute, spiritually.

The Poet's Commentary

Indeed, everyone has a past. And the production is a revelation of mine. Yes, I have moved on in life and gotten older. But the days of my youth were wild and eccentric ones inspired by my unconventional upbringing.

PERFECTION ELUDES ME.

I am not a perfect individual by any measure, and I've never presented myself as such. I'll be the first one to testify about my flaws—physical and otherwise—without shame.

As human beings, we all fall short. Not one of us gets it right all the time, and none of us ever will. We have all succumbed to something. We have all been slaves to something of sinful nature. And for this reason, not one of us can stand in judgment of another. We can speak by way of observation, sure, but not as judges.

STATING MY CASE.

What is an example of observation? One might ask.

Well, let's take a few of my productions, for instance. *The Falsifier, The Proverbial Diva,* and *Inspired by Imitation of Life* are all witnesses based on *spiritual observation* and not judgment.
They were inspired by what I had been *observing* in certain peoples' lives and actions. The works are not (meant to be) judgmental, but only to shed light on perversities based upon what I had been observing from a personal standpoint.

If it quacks like a duck, it's a duck. And people will address it accordingly. If it barks like a dog, it's a dog. And people will call it as such. If it growls like a bear, it's a bear. And you'll know it by its fruits.
The same scenarios apply here. You're not judging either creature; you're only referring to them by what they are, based on their characteristics.
The Testimony of Cat Ellington is a condensed account of my (personal) witness.
It reveals only a small portion of what my life had once been like when I lived it like a wild young woman of the world. It is not something that I gleefully endorse, but it was what it was. And I do not live with regret in the present because I cannot go back in time and change anything. Furthermore, I

believe that my former life had to be what it was yesterday for me to be the woman—in Christ—that I am today.

I do not point my index finger at anyone, lest my thumb should direct itself back towards me. But know this, that before I speak about *anything* concerning another person's trials, I will most definitely snatch the curtain back to reveal my own first. Always remember that. Because a hypocrite I have never been, nor ever will be. And I'm proud of that fact.

"The Windows Have Eyes"
Genre: Dark

The Synopsis

This production of the written word, in poetic form, intends
to witness the subject's descent into the deep throes of severe
depression and a yearning for death by suicide.
Here, the eyes are the windows of a tormented soul; the
downpour rain is the tear of scalding-hot emotional pain; and
the house, the physical body of entrapment.

The Poem:

The hellish abyss,
Dark and cold,
It bargains with time,

To lay hold on my eternal soul—

Every day, I battle with the shadows,
With things unseen:
Misery is consuming me,
Like the maggot on a corpse
That is my inner being—

Behind the velvet face,
There lies only moth-eaten decay:
O let death finally come,
Let it come,
I solemnly pray—

From the windows of my house,
There is a torrential downpour of rain—
Yet there is no one
Who can comprehend my inner pain?

I groan all alone—
And this hand I have been dealt?
I detest and bemoan—

Thoughts of self-destruction corrode me;
They corrode every layer of my hopeless psyche—

Lonely is my pitiable place;
No one cares about me—
Worse is that I'm awake:
Oh, how I wish that I could sleep—

If only I could fall asleep,

Then my soul would be free—
Free from the burden
That is my tormented body—

Behind the velvet face
There lies only moth-eaten decay:
O let death finally come,
Let it come,
I solemnly pray—

The hellish abyss,
Dark and cold,
It bargains with time,
To lay hold on my eternal soul.

The Poet's Commentary

Low self-esteem, self-hatred, self-pity, depression, hatred, anger, impatience, frustration, and irritation: they all may sound like simple words, but they're anything but simple.

THE (SPIRITUAL) EMANCIPATION OF ME.

They are *demons*. And they are real. And their primary purpose is to trouble the mind by tempting human beings to absolutely hate their own lives, to absolutely hate themselves, and to absolutely hate others. No one man, woman, or child possesses a monopoly on any of these as their spiritual warfare on human beings is universal. These tempt and trouble the minds of people all around the world – of every tongue, tribe, and nation. And they're dangerous.

I had fallen prey to the vicious (spiritual) assaults waged on my mind by these demons in my life once. And it took me many years to learn how to battle back against them (by way of divine rebuke).

For they had nearly cost me my life on several occasions, and I know each one of them quite well.

The Living Word is Truth:

"Resist the devil, and he will flee from you."
—James 4:7

Rebuke him in the name of Jesus, my dear men and women. And he'll get off of you. Trust me, I know.

Stay in hope, stay in faith, and stay in love. Keep your joy.

"The Proverbial Diva"
Genre: Satirical

The Synopsis

This production of the written word, in poetic form, intends to witness the great proverb of how hastily received inheritances come to nothing in the end. And of how pride will always precede a great fall.

The Poem:

Before her downfall,

She'd come into great means—
Because fame came quickly,
She'd come into great means...

Oh, she'd had it all—

Before her downfall,

She sang like a lovely dream—
The epitome of renown and esteem,
She sang like a lovely dream…

Oh, she'd had it all—

Before her downfall,

She'd reigned supreme—
A first-rate, world-class celebrity,
She'd reigned supreme…

Oh, she'd had it all—

Before her downfall,

The world had been at her "well-heeled" feet—
In a shameful display of false idolatry,
And unfathomable sycophancy,
The world had been at her "well-heeled" feet…

Oh, she'd had it all—

Before her downfall,

She'd arrogantly scoffed at humility—
Enveloped in the festivity of drunken revelry,
She'd arrogantly scoffed at humility,
And shunned the great Deity of Divinity…

Oh, she'd done it all—

Before her downfall.

The Poet's Commentary

The Proverbial Diva is my "You're So Vain".

Read into the piece whatsoever you will, dear reader.
Read into the piece whatsoever you will.

Part Three

"Enemy Centered"
Genre: Prose

The Synopsis

This production of the written word, in poetic form, intends to witness an evil trial of malicious hostility inflicted upon the subject—resulting from hatred, anger, racism, bigotry, and revenge.
Here, the "little birdie" serves to represent callous and embittered people.

The Poem:

You're gonna fly away, little birdie:
One of these days, little birdie,
One of these days, little birdie,
You're gonna fly away from me—

For you, little birdie, are of an adversarial coop;
Yes, you, little birdie, are of an adversarial coop—

But you're gonna fly away, little birdie:
One of these days, little birdie,
One of these days, little birdie,
You're gonna fly away from me—

(Chirp, Chirp)
You peck at me—
(Chirp, Chirp)
You're an evil trial, little birdie—
(Chirp, Chirp)
But one of these days, little birdie,
(Chirp, Chirp)
You're gonna fly away from me—

You're gonna fly away, little birdie:
One of these days, little birdie,
One of these days, little birdie,
You're gonna fly away from me.

The Poet's Commentary

The production was inspired by me enduring over seven years of hell on a popular social media platform.

THEY PECK WITH THEIR BEAKS.

This social media platform subjected me—without just cause—to nothing but anger, hatred, malice, racism, bigotry, covetousness, envy, jealousy, lust, spite, stalking, and harassment - from the top (the head of the company) on down through the lower ranks of said platform and out into the general public.

WHY I HAVEN'T FLOWN THE COOP.

I remained on this platform because I had every right to use it for networking purposes – just like everyone else does. It is a public social network. And during my time on it, I have never done anything deserving of the hatred that I have gotten. You know, from the people who control the site. My only offense—as far as these people are concerned—is the fact that I exist and that I can exist without having to kiss their asses or conform to what *they* believe I should be. I did my very best to make the most of my time on the social network in question since I signed up in 2012. But God, it has been an awful experience.

I say this because it had not been the platform itself, but rather the *people* thereon. The site is just that, a site. It could not harm. But the people operating it? *They* are the problem. The people utilizing it? *They* are the problem. The idiotic and self-loathing ass man serving as that company's CEO? *He*, especially, is the problem.

EXPOSING THE STUPIDITY.

The social network about which I speak is truly representative of a vile and perverse culture - brimming with all manner of confusion and madness. A loathsome social network chock full of hateful and ugly-spirited people: both the Jew and Gentile alike; both the well-known and unknown.

Using this particular social media platform has been nothing short of a terrible experience for me. And should the Lord allow me to live to 100 years of age, I will still be testifying about it. Not ever will I grow weary of testifying about it. Not ever. It has been a horrible experience with horrible people.

The social media platform about which I speak? It is a desperate place. And it crawls with desperate people who clamor too much. And for what? Pitiful and pathetic people who covet notability for doing absolutely nothing. Awful and bothersome and perverse people who jockey all over the damn place, trying in vain to grab hold of something for nothing. Lazy people who refuse to put in the hard-ass work one must do to acquire *LEGITIMATE* recognition and who can't help but hate (and envy) those that do: everyday people who shame themselves in desperate attempts to compete with PROFESSIONALS in the arts & entertainment industry.

It's just madness, what this pathetic system that needs to fuel the sorry ass engines of low self-esteem and self-hatred. Madness. I honestly cannot think of any other term to describe it.

And my personal experience with such madness over seven *long* years was just terrible. The social media platform about which I speak has been nothing short of unkind to several people—both renowned and unknown—so I am not the only one. But I needed to testify here concerning my (personal) experience on the site. It has also involved the "shadowing" of my name in my Mentions on the site, including several accounts claiming to be named *Ellington* when I know they're not. These are the same lying-ass people who deliberately tag the word *"cat"* in their posts so that they can have an excuse to troll the Mentions under my name. And the (hostile) people who operate the site have continuously denied me the option to "filter" my Mentions in the Settings feature.

Why? One might ask. Well, because a certain man at the company is also involved in the trolling. The CEO—with his nutty, obsessed, and troubled ass.

EXPOSING THE STUPIDITY FURTHER.

Now one might also ask: Cat, what has this man done that's so offensive?
'Quite a bit' would be my answer to the person.

As I mentioned earlier, the people who run the platform allow trolling because they, too, have become partakers in it. But the CEO? He is perhaps the worst one of them all. The man has gone so far as to use different variations of my name to create false accounts on the site to stalk and harass me. This repulsive man—out of unwarranted spite—also refuses to unlock my original username (inactive since 2012), so that I may be at liberty to reclaim it.

Moreover, my account on the site is still not verified because I refuse to kiss his skinny ass, validate his weak ass manhood, treat him as if he were my man (which he will never be), and pay him my hard-earned money for it.

When I joined this triflin' social network in 2012, ASCAP, Harry Fox Agency, and the Art Institute of Chicago had been three of the first accounts that I followed. That's how I know they were all there before me. And two-thirds of these profiles are *still* not verified? But many of these damn *YouTubers*—and nearly every one of these so-called "Reality Show personalities"—are?

Something is seriously wrong with that.

That is not hatred or envy speaking; it's the truth.

Something is seriously wrong with that.

People (and organizations), such as those mentioned above, should not have to pay for account verification on ANY social network - while illegitimate people dubbed as *Web stars* or *Internet famous* sit on these sites with unpaid ticks following their truly unknown names.

Are you reading these written words, Mr. CEO? Good, if you are. Because now you have a valid reason to call me *arrogant* and *narcissistic*, whereas you didn't before. You hateful, self-hating, angry, bitter, pathetic, abusive, power-hungry, and disturbed ass man you.

I know good-and-damn well you couldn't be that fuckin' enthralled with people like Lauryn Hill, Beyoncé, Kanye West, and Kendrick Lamar while you sittin' on yo' skinny, one-meal-a-day-eatin' ass throwing hate at me for no reason. If you're hostile (without cause) towards me, I know damn well you hate them because they're my people. We share a culture. You're full of shit, you're a damn liar, and the truth ain't nowhere near you.

You didn't win a friend in me; you only made an enemy of me. You keep that in mind. I sought to show kindness and friendship to you, but you couldn't even receive it because you're so damn full of fear, confusion, and self-hatred. Therefore, I withdrew my hand from you. And I will not extend it to you again. Now glare and frown at *that*, muthafucka. Don't seek an enemy in me, and you won't find one.

RESTATING.

Now, concerning my prior statements (regarding Payola for account verification), I feel like this. I have worked my ass off—as a creative writer—for decades. And whatever I'm blessed to receive on this Earth (as a result of my work), I want to be able to say that I genuinely EARNED—and NOT BOUGHT—it. And I do mean that with everything I have in me.

I have not worked in my craft, that is (creative) writing, for nearly 40 years of my life (building a catalog of work) to have muthafuckas—strangers at that—treating me as though I'm nothing, when I know good-and-damn well I am something. I know what my Lord has given me on this Earth of *His*. Therefore I will not bend and subject myself to the whims of a bunch of sorry-ass people. And neither should anyone else, be they public figures or members of the general public.

I have testified, time and again, about the hateful (and malicious) treatment I have endured as a member of the social network about which I speak. So the words spoken here are not foreign to those familiar with my postings at the *Boutique Domain* – the same that shed a bit of light on the situation. And because this personal trial of mine (spanning over seven years now) has been so unusually peculiar, I elected to compose a quick work of poetry in response to it; hence, *Enemy-Centered*.

ENCOURAGING OTHERS.

Many readers are sure to find this production highly relatable as they, too, might be encountering a similar experience, if not on a social media platform such as the one that inspired this work in some other area of their lives. Their troublers might be bosses or co-workers or schoolmates or even people with whom they live.
Whatever the situation, they're being given a hard time in their lives by self-hating and malicious people. But always remember this, that nothing lasts forever, not even your problems.

My dear men and women, here is a little bit of advice from me to you. When you see a storm coming towards you, don't turn and run away from it because it'll catch up with you in the same path. But when you see a storm coming towards you, run right through it. Because when you dare to run through a storm, it will eventually pass over you. It will pass over you, the sun will come out again, and your faith will be stronger for it. Always remember that, my dear men and women.

Stand in your faith.

God gotcha. Stand in your faith.

And also remember this, that God is. He has assigned every (human) dog his and her special day. And each one's day will be the most brutal. Always remember that. People will reap what they sow, be it for good or for evil. And the same outcome applies in every scenario of life. So be encouraged.

Nothing lasts forever.

Nothing.

Oh, and one more thing. In case some of you might be wondering why I cuss like I do, being as that I'm a Christian, pay heed:

While I may often cuss—in heated earthly-indignation, I am relentless in my obedience to the will of my Lord on this Earth. Indeed, I would run the soles off of my feet to obey my Lord's commandments. And He, in His almighty firmament, knows it. Should He command me to walk through a valley of deadly vipers, I would do so in a heartbeat because I know that He will not allow the venomous fangs of even one to strike me. But if hateful and evil-minded people allow themselves to break forth upon me, that they should mistreat me without cause, know for a certainty that I will cut their asses up with the verbal sword truth. And. I. Will. Not. Hesitate. *Not even for a moment.*

That is my answer to you.

You: But what about turning the other cheek, Cat?

Me: I have. That's why I ain't got no damn assault and
battery charges hangin' over my head.

"The Falsifier"
Genre: Satirical

The Synopsis

This production of the written word, in poetic form, intends to expose hypocrisy in those confessing to be members of the household of faith but whose actions are quite contrary to their spoken words.

The Poem:

I know of such a man:

His mouth speaks of Pentecostal Christianity,
But his actions expose the truth,
Which is worldly-minded immorality—

I know of such a man:

His mouth speaks of self-respect and unity,
But his actions expose the truth,
Which are self-deprecation
And partiality—

I know of such a man:

His mouth speaks of peer praise,
And God-fearing modesty,
But his actions expose the truth,
Which are backbiting
And impropriety—

I know of such a man:

His mouth speaks of cultural harmony,
And gracious piety,
But his actions expose the truth,
Which includes selfish infighting,
And a blatant obsession with his celebrity—

I know of such a man:

His mouth speaks of holy devotion,
And fervent love,
But his actions expose the truth:

It is only the world he truly desires to be a part of—

Yes,

I know of such a man.

The Poet's Commentary

Falsifiers. They exist all over the world. But the sole
individual who serves as the inspiration for my production,
The Falsifier, is one of whom we all know publicly.
Regardless of his Pentecostal Christian faith, the individual is
allowing evil to tempt him. And he's not rebuking it.

FACEBOOK ~~FRIENDS~~ ENEMIES.

The person about whom I speak is being tempted in his silly
mind to "backslide," if you will. The enemy tempts this
individual to hate himself. He is also tempting him to hate his
life in Christ and to hate his spiritual calling. This man has
become malicious and hateful in his actions towards other
people, including those who supported his career. This man
has come to hate his community. He is also coveting love,
approval, and acceptance from the people in the world: for
he has become loathsome.
This man, the same man about whom I speak, is desperate to
be perceived as a worldly celebrity rather than as a servant of
God—first and foremost. Do not believe his lip service.

This man has shamed himself in the public eye and, most
importantly, in the sight of the Lord. I know this because I
once fell prey to his anger and hatred back in 2012/2013.
And it, too, had been a most loathsome and evil situation.

The succeeding witness explains what the enemy tempted him to do to me.

While I managed a Facebook profile back in late 2012, early 2013, I subscribed to an industry page for a television program hosted by this man. He was also the moderator of the game show fan page at the time. And while I haven't been an avid viewer of the game show since its earlier years on TV, particularly during the early to mid-1980s, I had, however, been a great admirer of the man, himself, and only subscribed to the page for that (singular) reason. I said I had been. I had been a great admirer of the man about whom I speak until he allowed the enemy to tempt him to carry out an evil action against me in due course.

To engage both his and the game show's fan base, this man presented a question to his subscribers and asked them to give the most popular answer coinciding with a survey poll. And I dared to offer my unique answer to the question—which it had been my right to do in the first place. As far as I was concerned, it was only a friggin' game show poll, and it was supposed to have been good fun. But when you're dealing with self-hating people—be they public figures or members of the general public—their malice towards others will always get exposed eventually. And the man about whom I speak is one of such types, what self-hating. This man is full of self-hatred, not to mention hatred, anger, malice, and revenge towards other people. And he is being tempted to use his precious *celebrity* as a pathetic ass clutch. But when he ran his country-fried ass into me, he ran into the wrong woman.

The Wrong Woman. That sounds like it could be the title of a Lifetime Movies movie. Doesn't it?

Speaking of Lifetime Movies—formerly known as LMN—the legendary cable network is one of my most beloved channels - ever. And I have never been shy about voicing it publicly. By now, many of you know how much I adore the film projects that air on the Lifetime Movies network. And my passionate love for these films nearly got my Facebook account suspended all those years ago. Because I had the nerve to find joy in something, a certain someone sought to do what was evil to me. Indeed, his feet—clad in those ugly ass shoes of his—swiftly ran to do evil. And not once did his stupid ass stop to consider the consequences. You know, regardless of his tired-ass celebrity status, this individual is one of the miserable ones. He is a hateful and vindictive man who comes from a past of wretchedness. And he, despite the divine mercy that the Lord has shown him, has never forgotten it.

I will now make my point.

While I do not remember the question asked verbatim, it had gone along the following lines:

Ladies, other than his old age, name a reason you would want to marry a rich man?

The answers poured in. And mine had pertained to something that included LMN (the acronymic identity of the network at that time). No harm meant on my part. I was only having a little fun with my answer. But two days later, after signing in to my Facebook account, I returned to the game show page (to which I subscribed), saw another question asked, and typed out my answer. But when I clicked Post to share it to the thread, I was immediately greeted with the following bulletin: *You have been reported for spam.*

The dark pink notification threw me for a loop because (1) I did not know what the hell spam was, and (2) I could not think of any deliberate offense that I had committed against any other Facebook user. But after it settled in, the Holy Spirit immediately showed me who it was that had contacted Facebook to bring the spiteful charge against me: the game show host.

And the Holy Spirit, the Spirit of Truth in whom there is no lie found, did not make a mistake. This man had allowed himself to carry out a lowdown action against me out of spite. And why? Well, because I had spoken what I thought were words of encouragement to his ol' country, boxy suits-wearin' ass only a few days before I replied to the fateful question on the game show page. And I guess he didn't like what he heard, seeing that he was already acting like a rebellious backslider anyway. So he went behind my back and sought an opportunity to be vindictive towards me. And contacting Facebook to have my account flagged had been his chance.

What he did to me was lowdown. And if the Lord ever allows me to see his veneers-wearin' ass up close, I'm sure gonna tell him as much – straight to his face.

What he did to me, I could never have done to anyone and been able to sleep. My conscience would have eaten me up. But his ol' baldheaded, droopy-eyed ass slept, even after he did what was evil. He did what he did because he believed that his celebrity somehow made him immune.

Being new to the Internet and its social networks at that time, I had no understanding of what spam was, so I went into research mode. It was my job to know what it was that had accusations brought against me. And I spent the next four hours of that day reading through every page of the company's Policies and Guidelines. I even visited its forums to learn as much as I could about this thing called spam. And by the time I completed my research, I knew everything I needed to know.

Under the circumstances of my reply to the game show's original question, I had not committed any offense; nevertheless, I had offended the triflin' ass game show host, personally. And he contacted the company to utter a lie on me – in the hope that he would get my account suspended.

My account never suffered a suspension, but I learned a lot about the true nature of people. And in this case, the knowledge I gained had been from that of a well-known public figure who puts on his "God-fearing" airs in the faces of his "adoring" public, while his private actions are a blatant contradiction to the lip service he renders.

But one who sows shall also reap, whether for good or evil. And that goes for every one of us.

IMPATIENTLY WAITING.

No one is perfect. We all fall short. But when one knows better, the penalty for that person will be more severe than for people who do not know any better. And the man about whom I speak knew better. His ol' loud, black ass knew better. But he acted lowdown anyway. And I cannot wait for the opportunity to finally see his Uncle-Tomin ass up close so that I may be at liberty to tell him as much.

Now, it is not my intention to get physically violent with the man; I will not put my hands on anyone. But I am going to tell him how I felt about his lowdown-ass actions against me. *That*, I am going to do.

His public claim is this: *God has given me all that heart could wish*. But he sure doesn't act like it. Ain't no humility in his ignorant ass, only vindictiveness. And trust that I will most definitely tell him the same to his goofy-ass face the minute I see him up close and personal. Lord knows that day ain't comin' fast enough.

"Welcome to Springtime"

Genre: Minnesang

The Synopsis

This production of the written word, in poetic form, intends to pay tribute to what has to be the greatest affection known to Mankind, even that which is love.

Here, the subject joyously expresses its rapture.

The Poem:

I'm just smilin'...

I'm so happy,
I'm just smilin'...

I feel so blessed,

So wonderfully blessed—
So blessed, Oh, yes,
So blessed by the best—

And ah, the joy,
The beautiful joy—
Oh boy, oh boy,
I'm so full of joy—

You wanna know why?
You wanna know why?
Good gosh, oh my,
I'm tellin' you why—

It's 'cause I'm in love,
I'm madly in love—
I'm glowin' because
I'm madly in love—

This very first time,
My life is just fine—
Thank Heaven above;
I'm madly in love—

I'm happy and giddy and joyful,
Because—it's happened to me,
I'm madly in love—

I'm just smilin'...

I'm so happy,
I'm just smilin'.

The Poet's Commentary

And there you have it, folks. There is simply something amazingly gorgeous about the power of love. Love. It's a beautiful thing. And falling head over heels in it? Well, that's even more wonderful. Stay in love, and you'll stay empowered. Stay in love (and not in hate), my dearest men and women.

"The Golden Goose"
Genre: Satirical

The Synopsis

This production of the written word, in poetic form, intends to personally testify of one's own loathsome experience with those motivated by greed and covetousness, even the same who flatter to the face in the hope of gain.

The Poem:

Meet the woman who has great possessions:

I can do no wrong, no wrong at all,
And those around me are at my every beck and call—

Whatever I say or do, even if crooked and untrue,

They all love it
Because they all covet—

At every one of my stale jokes, they all laugh—
They all laugh because they covet what they do not have—

Meet the woman who has great possessions:

Seeking favoritism, they compete to tickle my ears:
Eagerly speaking to me only what I may desire to hear—
For these are a loathsome and miserable lot,
Who secretly plot to receive what I've got—

Meet the woman who has great possessions:

Yea, their flatteries to my face will eventually give way—
To bitter hearts filled with rot and decay—
But lest there shall befall me extreme economic plight,
I will continue to shine,
Within their ravenous eyes,
Radiantly bright—

Meet the woman who has great possessions.

The Poet's Commentary

Trust, my dearest reader, that you will know true friendship when you happen upon it. But beware of those who flatter to the face in the hope of gain.

Beware of the man-pleaser and the sycophant. And remember this wisdom:

The first person who will stick a knife in your back is an ass-kisser, considering that they are already (positioned) behind you.

"The Hour of Trial"
Genre: Dark

The Synopsis

This production of the written word—in poetic
form—intends to witness severe depression, anguish,
distress, frustration, rage, and self-loathing plaguing the
author as she wallows in a sea of self-pity during her hour of
intense, spiritual trial.
Here, she takes the plea of repentance before the Lord thy
God while the reader bears witness.

THE SPIRIT OF DEPRESSION WROTE THIS:

When the human spirit gets broken, hopelessness appears to
rejoice. I had once dared to lament in the wallowing of my
pitiful descent. My soul is pulling away from me like death

at harvest. For even it has waxed wary of the stranger that I have come to be.

This life You have given me, I have come to hate. And the people You made, I have come to hate. What has become of me? For I am deathly and sickly: open your mouth, Earth, and swallow me.

The Poem:

What has become of me?
What happened to the person that I used to be?

The free spirit is no longer;
For it too has bid me adieu—

Now, I am only a hardened shell:
A shell laid along the endless shores of a living hell.

What has become of me?
What happened to the person that I used to be?

The free spirit is no longer;
For it too has bid me adieu—

Now, I am only a hardened shell:
A shell laid out along the endless shores of a living hell.

An embittered soul, unloving and cold,
I search for the warmth of a lost love from of old—

What has become of me?

What happened to the person that I used to be?

The free spirit is no longer;
For it too has bid me adieu.

The Poet's Commentary

Trust, my dearest reader, that this has been (or will be) the lamentation of every brand new creature in Christ Jesus on the face of this great Earth.

THE FAITH TEST.

In the wake of making the born-again confession, there is always this thing called the bliss period. But once that bliss period ends and trials and tribulations begin, that is when people find out who they are. That's when Old Scratch is allowed to attack one's faith in God.

Are you going to remain faithful? Or are you going to turn back like Lot's wife?

A person will either stand in his or her faith in God—despite the growing opposition from Satan through ungodly people in the world system—or he or she will be defeated in (spiritual) battle and give up.

Me? I elected to stand in my faith and obey the Lord and His commandments. Because I wanted to be a true warrior, and I wanted to get the victory, and I wanted to receive the promise, and I wanted to see my dreams—even the ones I have had since the time that I was a very young child—become a reality. Therefore, I held on and fought against the old temptations that troubled me when I had been another lost soul plugged into the Matrix of the world system.

Those early years were rough, yes, but boot camp training will - in all due time - strengthen any soldier, including the spiritual boot-camp training designed for soldiers in Christ. Take off the old (man), and put on the new man. Take off the old (man), and put on the new man. It takes practice, but practice makes perfect.

Therefore, stand. And after having done all, stand.

Part Four

"The Adorable Rufus Hunter"

Genre: Friendship

The Synopsis

This production of the written word, in poetic form, intends to pay an affectionate tribute to a special friend and fellow Sagittarian, namely Rufus "Big Ru" Hunter.
Psst! You mah boy, Ru.

The Poem:

I adore you, Big Ru,
I adore you, I do—

You remind me of,
You remind me of a ray of sunshine:
The kind of sunshine that gleams,
The kind of sunshine that is bright,

The kind of sunshine that pries into the depths,
The depths of my dusky brown eyes—

I adore you, Big Ru,
I adore you, I do—

You remind me of,
You remind me of a warm, gentle breeze:
The kind of warm, gentle breeze that is carefree,
The kind of warm, gentle breeze that flees,
The kind of warm, gentle breeze that blows
With sweetly-succulent and effervescent ease—

I adore you, Big Ru.
I adore you, I do—

You remind me of,
You remind me of a peaceful night's sleep:
The kind of peaceful night's sleep that is tranquil,
The kind of peaceful night's sleep that is deep,
The kind of peaceful night's sleep that is rejuvenating
And serene,
Even to the inner core of the physical being—

I adore you, Big Ru.
I adore you, I do—

You remind me of,
You remind me of a smooth jazz melody:
The kind of smooth jazz melody that is sexy,
The kind of smooth jazz melody that is groovy,

The kind of smooth jazz melody that is mellow and moody—
You feelin' me, cutie?

Jazz—with all that pizzazz
To you from me—in a spirit of sultry sensuality—

I adore you, Big Ru.
I adore you, I do.

The Poet's Commentary

And I do love you, Ru. Thank you for being a friend.
Sagittarius forever, baby. Sagittarius forever!

"Mother Chicago"
Genre: Lyric

The Synopsis

This production of the written word, in poetic form, intends to witness the woes of a beautiful American city in horror. *Mother Chicago* was inspired by CNN's *Chicagoland*.

The Poem:

Mother Chicago,
You need to heed!
Embrace true wisdom,
And get understanding—

Mother Chicago,
You're draped in disgrace:
Your wounds are bleeding all over the place—

Mother Chicago,
It's time to erase,
It's time to erase every scar from your face—

Mother Chicago,
You need to heed!
Embrace true wisdom,
And get understanding...

Mother Chicago,
It's not yet okay,
You're losing your children to crime every day—

Mother Chicago,
You need to heed!
Embrace true wisdom,
And get understanding—

Mother Chicago,
Your prayers are a sin,
Your houses are laid-up with bloodthirsty men—

Mother Chicago,
The wicked endorse it,
They have no regard,
And they shun law enforcement—

Mother Chicago,
You need to heed!
Embrace true wisdom,

And get understanding...

Mother Chicago,
I want you to hear me,
I want you to hear me,
I love you so dearly—

Mother Chicago,
You need to heed!
Embrace true wisdom,
And get understanding.

The Poet's Commentary

Where's mine?
The corruption motto of Chicago—since 1869

Debilitating cancer eats away at its core, and it did not develop overnight. And one work of poetry is not a surefire way to make it alright. It takes an entire community to rebuke a culture of iniquity. And only one faithful chance to take a life-changing stance.

Need I say more?

"I Call the Wind Mariah Carey"
Genre: Lyric

The Synopsis

This production of the written word, in poetic form, intends to witness the great faith of the author in a long-awaited divine prophecy. A lyrical piece, this work graciously expresses her undying love for the one prophetic, even the inimitable Mariah Carey.

The Poem:

From her throat,
There came a musical sound.
'Twas a great wind that caused astound.
This ode to her is one most honorary.
I call the wind ... Mariah Carey.

You and I are prophesied
And highly favored in His eyes—
By the Lord, we were ordained
Kindred spirits in His name—
I love you with everything,
With everything within my being—
There has never been a day,
When through my mind, you didn't sway—

This is you,
I speak of you,
And from a spirit just and true—

This is you,
I speak of you,
My sister from another womb...

For many years I have been waiting,
Waiting and anticipating,
For us two, yes, me and you,
To be bonded through-and-through—
By the Lord, we were ordained
Kindred spirits in His name—
And His will I wish to do,
I am not ashamed of you—

This is you,
I speak of you,
And from a spirit just and true—

This is you,
I speak of you,

My sister from another womb...

You are now within my heart,
And from it, you will never part—
Trust His word will come to pass,
And we will be an everlast—

This is you,
I speak of you,
And from a spirit just and true—

This is you,
I speak of you,
My sister from another womb.

From her throat,
There came a musical sound.
'Twas a great wind that caused astound.
This ode to her is one most honorary.
I call the wind ... Mariah Carey.

The Poet's Commentary

God gives wisdom, even to the unlearned. One of whom I
had been way back in 1990, the year that He sent to me the
first vision concerning her.

Yeah, I had a vision, too. And it was a beautiful vision that,
to this very day, I still believe, even with everything I have in
me.

I still believe.

CHRISTMAS EVE, 1990.

I sat on the king-size bed in the luxury hotel room that I shared with one of my exes, "Mr. Saks Fifth Avenue," watching a rerun of the *Arsenio Hall Show* and eating imported cheese. My beloved ex, "Mr. Saks Fifth Avenue," was given that playful moniker because he was a Saks man. All of his tailored suits (quite a few) were Saks Label. And he took great pride in them: Mr. Saks Fifth Avenue took great pride in everything he had. He was just that type of guy: he worked hard, and he played hard. And I loved his soul.

Anyway, finally making time for a little R&R, he booked us a suite at the Radisson. We were going to spend the entire Holiday week just chilling out and eating and drinking and watching TV and being lazy and doing all of the other extracurricular activities that we enjoyed. Indeed, we were going to have a good time. And while I watched a commercial on our large TV, he prepared to order up more room service. We first discussed the menu items that we were going to order, and then he made the call. And it was while he placed our orders with RS that Arsenio resumed. The dearly beloved (and legendary) comedian/late-night show host was introducing his next guest, a new songstress named Mariah Carey - who was about to perform her popular debut single, "Vision Of Love." And it may have been while she was belting out the second verse that the

Holy Spirit spoke the following words into my mind: *She is going to be like a sister to you one day, Cat.*
My internal response to that? *Oh, okay.*

Though spoken loud and clear in the spirit, the words—about this woman from New York whom I knew not—fell on deaf ears as I couldn't care less. And being the self-absorbed girl that I was during that time, I moved on with the evening, not once considering the thought that had entered my mind earlier any further: for I floated in my own orbit and didn't want anyone else in my space.

THE SANDS OF TIME.

The Lord would speak to me about the slim and curly-haired girl again and again as time progressed. Over three decades later, He would still be talking about the pretty gal via divine prophecies and visions. And that is the truth. The Lord has never ceased to speak to me about this woman. He has chosen her to be a part of my life. For according to His words, which will surely come to pass, she is my kindred spirit and my sister from another mother.

At the time of this writing, it has been nearly 30 years since the first vision was shown to me on that fateful night in the hotel room. And over time, I became compelled to believe every prophetic utterance, no matter how long each prophecy seemed to be taking to come to pass. That is called faith, my dearest men and women. Real faith. And my faith has had no other choice but to grow over the years. While she is still *eternally 12*, I have gotten a lot older, spiritually. And because no one who is blind can lead the blind — lest they should both stumble over into a ditch — it was I who had to mature first, considering that I was converted to Pentecostal Christianity ahead of her.

THE UNUSUAL INTRODUCTION.

In April of 2012, about a month after I joined the Internet, I was guided by the Spirit to reach out to Mariah by way of an old social network outlet. The outlet about which I speak allowed its users to send text messages to other users to start a conversation thread. So here is what I did. I mustered up the courage (I was a nervous wreck at the time, y'all) and started a conversation with Mariah, typing out a short message and introducing myself. And as I received notification of each message sent, I typed out a few more, gaining more courage with each new letter. I was initially nervous because we were not face-to-face: I had only been communing with her via text messages. And I did not want her to think that I was some crazy whack job, you know? Everything was new to me then, the usage of the Internet. But thankfully, I'm a quick learner.

The text conversations lasted until April of 2014. I know this because I have every one of my letters to her copied on paper today and safely stored away in a binder. And if I might say as much, I gained a new fan in the woman named Mariah Carey during that time. But I am not surprised by that. Because she is an Aries, you know? And the Aries? Well, the Aries can't help but be fascinated with the Sagittarius.

(Laughs)

All good-natured jokes aside, know that I speak the truth, dearest reader. The woman named Mariah Carey is my number one fan. And I? Her biggest inspiration.

THE AFTERMATH.

Full of pride, ego, arrogance, and rebelliousness, she acted ugly in her ways and showed her ass on me for the first few years. And I had to inform her of my bullshit intolerance online, particularly at the Boutique Domain, via published postings. But despite our bumping heads due to any number of our differences, I love Mariah Carey more than any word in the English vocabulary can express. And I would go down fighting for her in a heartbeat if push came to shove. But I will not tolerate her infamous ass Divatude. *Not even for a split second.*

So, there you have it, my dearest men and women, what a summary of the events that inspired the production, *I Call the Wind Mariah Carey.*

And as for you, Ms. Carey? Get it real:

The Earth is spacious enough for both of us. And there is more than enough air for the two of us to share.

"I Am Cat Ellington"
Genre: Dramatic

The Synopsis

This production of the written word, in poetic form, intends to witness glory ascribed to the one and only Jehovah and His Christ through the declarative statement made by His deaconess, even the same called to be a creative artist on the Earth. That is I, Cat Ellington.

The Poem:

The one who has created me
From the dust of the Earth?
It is He whom I serve:

The one who has given unto me
The ability to speak wisdom
Through the written word?

It is He whom I serve:

The one who has brought me forth
To utilize me from within—
Like a double-edged sword?
It is He whom I serve:

Forever.

In the names of this Holy One
And of His only begotten Son?

I am— Cat Ellington.

The Poet's Commentary

Saturday, July 16, 1994

It was the day that I made up my mind to do things the right way. And my life has not been the same since.

Liberated.

"Wonderment"
Genre: Narrative

The Synopsis

This production of the written word, in poetic form, intends to witness the author, though alive and well, being treated as if dead by various people, but who, nevertheless, remains a challenge to ignore.

The Poem:

Here is what I perceive in my reality;
Here is what I perceive my reality—to be:

Why do they fear me?
Why do they not endear me?
Do they hate because they cannot relate?

Is it because I contradict their stereotypes?
Is it because I depict an original prototype?

Why do they fear me?
Why do they not endear me?
Do they hate because they cannot relate?

Ah, let the ear hear:

They hate—because they cannot relate—

Awe baffles the mind,
And the eye lays in its socket:

See—

In baffled awe,
They continue to watch me—

The muted mouth does not speak,
But the liquid eye can see,
The liquid eye can see me—

From afar, their actions are quite bizarre—

Here is what I perceive in my reality.
Here is what I perceive my reality—to be.

The Poet's Commentary

My dearest men and women, I felt compelled to testify about this for three specific reasons: to testify regarding my spiritual trial, to expose the lies, bigotry, racism, hatred, self-hatred, and vile hypocrisy in the world, and to speak to those experiencing a similar treatment in the world, so that they may be encouraged to continue onward in endurance and perseverance.

THE CULT OF ~~PERSONALITY~~ POPULARITY.

While the silly childishness and self-hatred of many of those who engage in social media activities on the Internet show themselves disapproved daily, I have elected not to participate in the madness with them. Because I know who I am. And thankfully, I do not need any of these people in the world to tell me who I am.

Get understanding, my dearest men and women. Once upon a time, worldly popularity and I had been quite close. Both it and I were well-acquainted, especially during my teen years into the era of my twenties. Indeed, wherever I ventured on land, popularity had its rightful place alongside me as we were inseparable. But on the day that I made the good confession and formed a new bond of friendship with the Divine Trinity, worldly popularity and I parted ways as it was inevitable. And while it still seeks to keep up with me today, even if only from a great distance, worldly popularity and I will never again be as close as we once were. And that is just as well as it carries the bulky weight of too many conditions.

I have to be me. That is just the way it is. And not everyone is going to be understanding of that. I have to be who I am and not who others want me to be. I have always been this way, but that has never stopped popularity from seeking me out, even to this very day. Unfortunately, the same is not the case for many people who covet popularity on social media platforms – seeing it as a cheap means to compensate for their low self-esteem. For example, lots of *Likes* equates to being *liked* by a lot of people, particularly strangers. While having lots of *Followers* equates to having a false sense of fame. For such people foster a desperate desire to receive honor and notability without producing any creative works. And lest I forget, photoshopped photos. These only serve to cater to a delusional mindset that tells many everyday people they are members of some professional industry—most likely entertainment or fashion—when in reality, they are anything but: for there lies the spirit of madness. And it will drive people to insanity if they find themselves void of understanding.

I do not need to strive for social media popularity. It simply is not that important to me. Because I already know popularity, it is not unfamiliar to me. As a young girl of only seventeen, I had my very own phone word. That is how closely associated with popularity I had been. It. Is. Not. New. To. Me.

As a (professional) creative artist in the arts & entertainment industry, I do not receive money based on likes and followers on social media platforms. As a (professional) creative writer in literature, I do not get money based on follower counts on social media platforms.

I see social media for what it is: networking, nothing more, nothing less. But if people view social media platforms as anything other than what they are or use them to obtain some false (and delusional) sense of renown—otherwise known as fame—something is wrong with that. And trust that low self-esteem, self-hatred, desperation, bitter envy towards others, racism, jealousy, greed, covetousness, idolatry, laziness, and hopelessness are all acting as the maniacal culprits.

A WOMAN WHO DARES TO BE CONFIDENT.

I am who I am, and I do what I do, even professionally. And I was who I am and doing my professional work long before there was such a thing as social media. And when this miserable and pathetic era dissolves into a new and much better era, I will still be who I am and doing what I do, even professionally.
Always remember that.

Time. It will most certainly reveal.

BE YOU. DO YOU.

My dearest men and women, peace, self-love, and contentment with oneself do not happen overnight. They are hard-won. And if I may suggest anything to you, it would be for you to have faith in God. Believe in yourselves. Love yourselves. Be at peace with others. And embrace the unique talents that you have. Work on developing your skills. And mind what is on your plate and not that of someone else. Do this, and you will be at peace.

Any lawn of grass can be lush, healthy, and a gorgeous shade of Kelly green if it is well cared for; therefore, you should nurture your abilities and be at peace. Because once people start comparing their own lives to the lives of others, hostilities are sure to arise, especially if they feel inferior or inadequate in comparison to the target of their envy.

Believe in yourself. And do not keep your dreams waiting lest they move on without you.

Rebuke fear. Conquer fear.

Part Five

"A Test of Character"
Genre: Prose

The Synopsis

This production of the written word, in poetic form, intends
to witness the author coming down to the end of her fiery
trials and tribulations.
Here, the spirit of the piece reflects humility, maturity,
gratitude, and reverence.

The Poem (Part I):

As I trek through this wilderness,
My heart comes to know the spirit of bitterness:

Am I not all alone?
Am I not all alone?

To Thy command to rebuke,
I have not been mute,
Nor have I given in to grumble
And refute—

Am I not all alone?
Am I not all alone?

Am I not cold?
And with each passing hour,
Am I not becoming a new day old?
Am I not in distress?
Am I not in distress—
As I trek through this wilderness?

Am I not all alone?
Am I not all alone?

Before Thee,
I have been humble;
And not a word against Thee
Have I ever mumbled:

For to Thee,
I have been obedient,
Lest Thou would not have been lenient...
With me—

The Witness (Part II):

For Thou had concealed me from the rain,
And relieved me of my emotional pain:

For Thou had sheltered me from the wicked storm.

Thou hast provided me with love from above,
And kept me warm in the storm:
For I had become distressed in the wilderness.

That every eye should see,
After Thou hast delivered me,
The great honor and mercy
Thou hast bestowed upon me—

Then there will be no more distress.

The Poet's Commentary

Trials and tribulations are no sunshine day at the park. Trust me when I tell you that, my dearest men and women. One to whom much is given, much is required. And I have been chosen to do a prolific work on the Earth – both spiritually and creatively; therefore, my spiritual trial had to be extended over several years, that my mind should be well-trained and equipped for service in honor of the King. For this prolific work that I am ordained to do is not my will but that of the Lord. And I must do His will to the best of my human ability.

My dearest reader, I composed *A Test of Character* while I had been going through a very rough period in my life and felt like my spirit was at the point of breaking altogether. And although that chapter of my life has ended, many others are currently in the training stage. And I want to encourage everyone to remain at their posts and complete their (spiritual) training. Because I have been there and know what the barracks are like, I encourage you to stand your ground, soldiers. Rebuke the enemy away from you in the name of Jesus, and stand in your faith. Conquer the old (man) and overtake him with the new man. Stay in that spiritual school and do not drop out. Pass those faith tests and earn your honors. Get. Your. Blessings! Do you understand me? Get your blessings!

The enemy will do everything he can to tempt you to drop out, but you better not drop out. You stay in the boot camp, complete your spiritual training, and open your mouth wide so that the Lord may fill it with blessings you shall not have room enough to receive. Stay in the Faith. Trials do not last forever. It only seems that way while you're going through them. Always remember that.
Stand in your faith. And be of good courage. It will be over before you know it. And you'll look back at the trial and laugh. Trust me, I know. Stand in your faith. And be blessed. I love y'all.

"Luxury"
Gogyohka

The Synopsis

This production of the written word, in the subgenre of micropoetry, intends to witness the peaceful state of contentment.

The Poem:

The warmth of your arms
Wrapped around me?
I liken them to this:
A gentle cashmere sweater
That comforts me in the winter.

The Poet's Commentary

Although *Luxury* is not one of my favorite works, I decided to include it in this book anyway. After all, it was (partially) inspired by one of my favorite cashmere sweaters, a cute little V-neck number in a lovely plum shade. The piece—centered around a lover's embrace—was also composed on a whim: I scribbled the very first words that came to mind.

But regardless of how I feel about the work, my dearest readers, I hope you all will find some enjoyment in it.

"Beastial"

Gogyohka

The Synopsis

This production of the written word, in the subgenre of micropoetry, intends to witness ruthlessness among men.

The Poem:

They break forth
Upon men
Like lions
Full of bloodthirst,
Annihilating their prey.

The Poet's Commentary

The truth follows.

A BREAKDOWN OF SORTS.

Now, this is what happens when people hate other people. But before they can hate others, they must first hate themselves. Worse is when such people are in positions of power, authority, and influence. Indeed, they become abusive to others - and a terror to themselves: for such people are open wells filled up with all manner of evil and ungodliness. There is not even one man, woman, or child on Earth who has not encountered the "wrath" of these people at some point in their lives. Wicked people—such as the ones about whom I speak—never last long though, it only appears that way. But while they're awake—meaning alive—they pose themselves as an evil trial unto other human beings with no qualms. However, in the very hour of their perishing, the people will rejoice.

These are great bywords - even great examples of how one must not live his or her life on Earth, what being a wicked hindrance unto others through systemic oppression, financial warfare, physical violation, dishonest scales, discriminatory practices, etc. These are weights with which wicked people burden the poor, the working-class, the needy, the fatherless, and the widow: for theirs is the law of the evil one, and it is his bidding that they eagerly do. But only for a season. For a little while, they are allowed to fester in their wickedness before they're cut down and diminished forever. And if one so desires to search out their place, he or she shall not be able to locate any place for them.

For the way of such wicked individuals is eternal death. And the spirit therein is *Beastial*.

"Hot and Humid"

Tanka

The Synopsis

This production of the written word, in the subgenre of micropoetry, intends to witness erotica.

The Poem:

He drips profusely:
His manhood inside of me,
Stretching and filling
My wide-opened cavity—
He whispers to me, saying...

The Poet's Commentary

There is simply no art better than that of lovemaking: for it is indeed my most undeniable pleasure. and in it, I take great solace.

Erotic pleasure. One of the most delectable pastimes of life.

"We Love You!"
Senryu

The Synopsis

This production of the written word, in the subgenre of micropoetry, intends to refer to the blazing glare of the media and the harsh cutty public eye reminiscent of the adage, *They build you up to tear you down.*

The Poem:

The lens of bitterness
Is an eye of hate:
It cuts through the mind and soul.

The Poet's Commentary

More truth.

THINKING BACK.

I can remember reading an interview that a writer for *Ebony* magazine had done with the late, great Whitney Houston many years ago – in which Whitney shared a little bit of wisdom that had been passed down to her by her legendary mother, Cissy. Those words of wisdom had pertained to the following:

'Nippy, the perfume is only meant to be smelled, not drunk.'

Whitney went on to interpret the meaning of her mother's advice, telling the interviewer—in so many words—that they pertained to both the spotlight of fame, the media, and the general public – whose sugar-coated sweetness in the beginning often turns sour like vinegar in the end. The clear-cut meaning of the parabolic advice that Cissy Houston shared with her beloved daughter? *'They build you up to tear you down.'*
I don't know about anyone else who may have read that fascinating interview from the late 1980s, but I took those words of wisdom to heart—literally—as if they had been spoken to me by my mother, a wise woman in her own right. And they're still written on the tablet of my heart today, even after all these years.

Only smell the perfume, don't drink it.

When one is doing work in public, especially if that work is considered high-profile, it's best to keep a level head and remember who you are as the ego is a natural trait common to all people. And in the case of those wise words, the incomparable Cissy Houston spoke to her equally storied daughter, Whitney: ego had been the trait to whom she referred.

We still see it today, the exaltation of celebrated people from both the media and public-at-large. Everything floats along just fine until the celebrity makes the mistake of being human and says or does one little "offensive" thing. From there, the media—as a collective body—goes to work churning the instigation machine to sway public opinion about that person to the negative side of the fence. And before long, down he or she goes. Because the public is fickle and very rarely is true loyalty found in them.

In a nutshell, that was the point of my short piece, the same being *We Love You!*

Thank you, Mrs. Houston, for speaking the truth to your child. Because when she repeated those words publicly, they went on to be a great blessing to others, including myself, as I have never forgotten them.

Part Six

"The Heavy Load"
Senryu

The Synopsis

This production of the written word, in the subgenre of micropoetry, intends to witness the hopelessness of a weary human soul.

The Poem:

In the depths of grief,
The spirit faints:
Here, it swelters in depression.

The Poet's Commentary

This piece takes its inspiration from my battle with depression and suicidal tendencies.

I'M A SURVIVOR.

While *The Heavy Load* was originally a fuller piece (written when I was 15), I elected to shorten the work and publish it as micropoetry in 2013. I believed that the composition, in its edited form, would be enough to serve its purpose. And I hope that it has.

To those of you out there who can relate to my witness, I say be of good courage and overcome. You are going to be okay, and you are going to make it. Believe that. You are going to do just fine. Believe me. All you have to do is reel in that pride and put it in subjection to you. Let go of it and let God handle it; because you cannot change one hair on your head. So just let all of that old mess go and live. Do you understand me? Let that old mess go and thrive. Let it all go and stay alive. Get yourself back in the race, run it, and win it!

"Jeer"
Gogyohka

The Synopsis

This production of the written word, in the subgenre of micropoetry, intends to witness hate-filled spirits of contempt.

The Poem:

The serpent
Uncoils itself,
Then slithers up
To hiss from
Throats of scoffers.

The Poet's Commentary

The scoffer and the wise are not the same.

DIFFERENTIATING THE TWO.

While a wise man will love you for supplying him with a cold drink of sound wisdom, that he should become wiser - a scoffer, on the other hand, will gnash his teeth at the truth and hate the one bearing it. Indeed, we have all had our share of encounters with the scoffer, even with one who is entirely faithless and whose throat is a well of strife. And if you desire to understand, you should know that it is written, 'Do not give what is holy to the dogs, nor cast your pearls before swine, lest they trample them under their feet, and turn and tear you in pieces.'

My dearest men and women, whenever you encounter an angry and contentious person in denial, trust that you have happened upon folly. Bite your tongue and go your way in peace lest you be scorched and consumed by the kindled flames of their self-destruction.

"ThatsStuff"
Genre: Dramatic

The Synopsis

This production of the written word, in poetic form, intends to witness an emotional testimony concerning my beloved mother and her battle with the demon called drug abuse.

The Poem:

She was a mighty dainty dame.
How was it that she began to lose her way?

That stuff is gon' kill her;
Lord, rebuke her dealer!
That stuff is sho gon' kill her;
Lord, rebuke her dealer!

I fear for her—

That stuff?
It took away her beauty—
That stuff?
It stole away her dignity—
That stuff?
It hindered all her ability—
That stuff?
It even drove her to poverty—

Dear Mama,

You're breaking my heart:

That monkey, dear Mama,
It's gon' tear us apart—

You need me, dear Mama,
And I need you—
But if you leave me, dear Mama,
What the hell am I gonna do?

Dear Mama—

The Poet's Commentary

I wrote this piece about my mother during her struggle with crack cocaine addiction in 2004. She spent time in rehab, and she is now well – both spiritually and physically.

Thank you, Lord God.

THAT'S MY MAMA.

Thank you, Mama, for allowing me to share your personal experience, in brief, with my reading public. Because it is for a certainty that others will be able to relate, even wholeheartedly, to our witness. I love you, Mama. And I am proud of you. You got the faith back, and I am so very proud of you. You are still a mighty dainty dame. And I love you all the same.

I got my Mama back. :)

"That Which Is Never Full"

Gogyohka

The Synopsis

This production of the written word, in the subgenre of micropoetry, intends to witness the symbolic terror of eternal destruction.

The Poem:

That which feeds
Into the mouth
Of the fiery pit
Is the main course
Of the lost soul.

The Poet's Commentary

The path of the wicked: it guides their crooked feet over the cliffs of Sheol.

THE PATH OF THE UNJUST.

Today they live, eat, drink and make merry while they inflict suffering upon others. But tomorrow, you will search out their places on Earth and not be able to find them anywhere: for theirs is a spiritual escalator that goes straight down into the spiritual realm.
See, preceding them were those of their generations before them. And know for a certainty that following them will be those of their lineage after them.

The piece, *That Which Is Never Full,* is intended to shed light on the way of the damned.

Live on this Earth long enough, and you will start to notice a pattern: there is always a price to pay when people do evil and be evil. And that goes for every man and woman of every tongue, tribe, and nation.
Get wisdom, my dearest men and women. Get wisdom.

"From One End to the Other"

Gogyohka

The Synopsis

This production of the written word, in the subgenre of micropoetry, intends to witness the double-minded.

The Poem:

These are the perverse:
Who shun and spurn
As they sway to,
And who flatter and cajole
As they sway fro.

The Poet's Commentary

I have always had the following mottos: (1) If you can't speak to me all the time, don't speak to me at all, and (2) If one is not willing to eat beans with you, the same is not worthy to eat steak with you.

These are my mottos, even ones that I have tended to live by since I was old enough to remember. And I have never faltered in my beliefs.

THE REAL DEAL.

When dealing with people, regardless of whomever they may be, I have always dealt with them straightforwardly. With me, what you see is what you get because I do not put on airs. And I am not a very good liar. If I like you, I will tell you as much. And I will tell you exactly why I do. I will not beat around the bush with you. But if I do not like you, trust that I will inform you of as much. And I will tell you exactly why I do not. I will not beat around the bush with you. That is the way I live my life, what straightforwardly. But not all share my level of bluntness.

IF I KNEW BACK THEN WHAT I KNOW NOW.

As a professional in the arts and entertainment industry, I finally decided to join a few social media platforms in 2012. I wanted to connect: with not only those members of the general public but also those of fellow creatives in the industry. And by the time of this writing, regret would still be gnawing at me because of that decision. For had I known then what I know now, I would never have reached out to any of them. But it had to happen. It had to be. Because I learned a valuable lesson from it: I had to be allowed to see people for who they (truly) are: a bunch of self-hating, miserable, bitter, angry, malicious, vindictive, faithless, hopeless, envious, and jealous-hearted people.

A BLUNT INSTRUMENT.

Here is something you all should know about me. After I have extended my hand in a spirit of kindness to anyone, and that person regards my hand with spite and hatred, I will never again offer my hand to the same person. Never again. I will leave them alone and let them be. Because they did not do it to me, they did it to the Lord, considering that I am His servant. Therefore, they do not have to answer me. But they will have to answer to Him. And He does not play with human beings that He made from dust – be they well-known human beings or unknown human beings. The Lord does not play with people who allow themselves to act hatefully. Trust me, I know.

When people—especially those who know better—allow themselves to heed the lies of the enemy rather than rebuking those lies away from their minds, it will not be good for them. And quite a few of the individuals to whom I reached out and got shunned know better. But sadly, they refused to do better.

Those about whom I testify are the same who claim to be members of one Body, even that of Christ. But they were tempted to act perverse and worldly-minded, thinking that their actions were going unnoticed. And rather than showing themselves approved, they preferred to settle in their ugly ways by engaging in partiality towards me, thereby conducting themselves like judges with evil thoughts. With their lips, they praise the name of the Lord before the people, but their hearts are full of bile. And though I may strongly desire to do so, I will refrain from mentioning any of their well-known names lest they should deny my witness and accuse me of slander. But they know who they are. And *I* know who they are. And one day, when desperation drives them to the other end of the spectrum, and they jockey to seek me out, so will you, my dearest reader. I will make sure of it.

HUMBLE YOURSELVES.

I am not willing to kiss the ass of anyone, and I do not expect anyone to kiss mine (and Lord knows I got way more ass than every one of 'em), but it would have been pleasing had they exhibited a little bit of self-respect while showing the same to others.

The people about whom I speak are not deities. They are only creative people who work in the entertainment industry. That is all. But many are delusional. They see their status in society as being anything other than what it truly is: a job. And when people start treating the job as though it is a false idol in which they put their faith, the same people are already on the wrong road.
It is just a job. And you folks do not have to act shitty with other people as a result of your either having—or having had—that job because I work in the same industry. I am a

member of various guilds and societies in the industry, too. And just because I am not seated at the same table with you breaking bread does not make me nonexistent or unimportant. If you pay attention, you will find out that the truth is the exact opposite. It just has not been revealed yet.

So watch yourselves because you may need me for something one day. And I will bet good money on the odds that most of you will.

Humble yourselves.

ONE FINAL JOLT.

That is the folly with people, you see? They know where they have been but do not know where they're going. They can remember what happened yesterday, but they don't know what's going to happen tomorrow. Be careful of nothing.

Part Seven

"The Bout"
Genre: Narrative

The Synopsis

This production of the written word, in poetic form, intends to witness a spiritual battle with the enemy, cast here as an "Opponent" in the symbolic setting of a boxing match. Here, great faith is what sustains the witness.

The Poem:

My opponent tries to beat me,
My opponent tries to defeat me,
My opponent tries to delete me,
My opponent tries to retreat me—

My opponent tries it all,

But to no avail—
Because my Trainer?
My Trainer has trained me well—

Even when the bell sounds,
Ding, ding, ding—
I'm still standing on both feet,
I'm still standing in the ring—

Even when the bell sounds,
Ding, ding, ding—
I still elude defeat,
I'm still standing in the ring—

Even after every round,
My opponent still can't keep me down—
Even after every uppercut,
I'm still standing up—
Even after every low blow,
My opponent still can't get a TKO—

I elude defeat,
I'm still standing on both feet—
I elude defeat,
I'm still standing on both feet—

My opponent fails to beat me,
My opponent fails to defeat me,
My opponent fails to delete me,
My opponent fails to retreat me.

The Poet's Commentary

In this order: humble yourself, repent of your sins, accept the Lord Jesus Christ as your personal Lord and Savior, receive the Holy Spirit of God in His name, make the Good Confession, take up your cross, and let the trials, tribulations, and public persecutions begin. Get the victory!

A GOOD TESTIMONY.

The Bout is my witness, respectively. And it was inspired by over 25 years of my membership in the Body of Christ. Dear fellow brethren, always remember this one thing while undergoing your spiritual trials: the enemy will throw everything he has at you until he uses up all of his evil tools, and you get the victory in the name of Jesus.
As the timeless song lyrics go, *The battle is not yours. It's the Lord's.*
And He has already won it. So be of good courage.

"And Now A Word From Chicago's South Side"

Genre: Narrative/Dramatic

The Synopsis

This production of the written word—in poetic form—intends to witness the author embodying a particular geographical location.

Here, if the South Side of Chicago could talk, it would say:

The Poem:

There is a mission to condition your minds against me:

You always hear about my so-called curse—
Because they have made it a habit
To only show me at my worst—

But you never get to see my beauty—
Because all they want to show you is my ugly...

There is a mission to condition your minds against me:

You always hear about my economic pain—
Because they have made it a habit
To only shine the spotlight on my maim—
And while they focus on my trepidation,
Never do they take the time to recognize
My great education...

There is a mission to condition your minds against me:

You never see my luxurious homes and condos—
Because they have made it a habit
To only publicize my crime-ridden ghettos;
And because I am—always—shown at my worse,
I am—forever—regarded among the scourge of the Earth...

There is a mission to condition your minds against me:

You never get to see my God-fearin'—
Because they have made it a habit
To only showcase those who're my wicked churen;
And though there be within me wisdom
That is second to none—
According to their witness,
All of my children are coming undone...

There is a mission to condition your minds against me:

You always hear about my so-called curse—
Because they have made it a habit
To only show me at my worst—
But you never get to see my beauty—
Because all they want to show you is my ugly...

And why?
So that you might be susceptible
To perceive me through the eye of a lie—

There is a mission to condition your minds against me.

The Poet's Commentary

From her, there is much Godly praise. And both she and her children? Well, they see many joyful days. Indeed, within her, there is tremendous hope. But is anyone ever allowed to hear about it? Nope.

WHY DO THEY HATE THE SOUTH SIDE OF CHICAGO SO MUCH?

Judged and spat at, pissed on, pooped on, and ridiculed: that is the South Side of Chicago. Mocked and excluded, ignored, scoffed at, lied about, and singled out: that is the South Side Of Chicago. Demonized and looked down, denigrated, redlined, and always used as a scapegoat: the South Side of Chicago.

But even still, she keeps going.

Despite the lack of a positive spotlight on her, even still, she shines. And although many feet ache from all the work they put in stomping her down, the Lord blesses her to keep rising. Because contrary to the lies they prefer to believe about her, God is for her. And He is with her. Because many, not all, but many of her children continue to stand in their faith in Him. And they have not bent the knee to the spirit of error in the world: for this reason, Satan, who operates through ungodly people, has waged war against her and her predominantly Black children, whom, by the way, just so happen to embrace Pentecostal Christianity in mass numbers: for the people are monolithic and unified in that regard. Therefore, a (spiritual) war wages against them. And it manifests itself in the godless and oppressive treatment that it inflicts upon them.

PREACH, GIRL!

The war has never been so much about the physical than it is about the spiritual. It was always a spiritual battle, even from day one: because the people chose to put their faith and trust in God, not in Man. And there lies the rage – operating through racism and economics.

Everyone is not asleep. Satan only tries to make it look that way.
Not all are lost. Satan only tries to make it look that way.
Not all are down and out. Satan only tries to make it look that way.
Not everyone is getting shot to death. Satan only tries to make it look that way.

Not all are broke and struggling. Satan only tries to make it look that way.
Not every neighborhood is dilapidated. Satan only tries to make it look that way.
Not every young Black man is a thug or gangbanger. Satan only tries to make it look that way.
Not every young Black girl is popping babies out of her ass at an alarming rate. Satan only tries to make it look that way.
Not every sidewalk is cracked up and caved in. Satan only tries to make it look that way.
And he uses many evil-minded people in the world—particularly in both politics and the media—to perpetuate his evil lies. For it was spoken concerning him, 'He is a liar and the father of it.' For the devil tempts those people—whose minds are open to his lies—to only seek out the worst in others, particularly in those who are African American.

By the way, whenever you hear someone say, *In the South Side* rather than *On the South Side,* know for a certainty that the same is an ignorant-ass outsider who does not know what the hell he or she is talking about: it's not *In* the South Side, dumb-asses, it's *On* the South Side.

Oh, and another thing. Contrary to popular belief, we have beautiful flowers, living trees, and green grass, too. We also have gorgeous parks, lovely bookstores, state-of-the-art libraries, fascinating museums, stunning art galleries, and cozy cafés.
We have beautifully decorated homes, and apartments, and high-end vehicles, too.

We have youth centers that cater to the advancements of our children, too.
You might not hear about them, but we do.

Be ye not deceived, my dearest men and women.
Be ye not deceived.

"This Womanhood"

Genre: Dramatic

The Synopsis

This production of the written word, in poetic form, intends to witness both the social struggles and spiritual triumphs of the Black woman in America.

Inspired by over four centuries of integrity.

The Poem:

We are strength...to the furthest extent;
We are queens—
Who descended from kings:

We have swam

In the oceans of hate—
Through the whip,
Through the branding and rape—
We withstood
Every torture and ache
From the ones who decided our fate—
We have suffered many wages of sin,
But survived
And we stood by our men—
We have borne many children in plight,
Swung the rod,
So they knew wrong from right—
We are blessed,
We don't settle for less—
How do we do it?
Well, that's anyone's guess—

We are strength...to the furthest extent;
We are queens—
Who descended from kings:

We have cried
Bitter tears from our eyes;
We were judged,
And subjected to lies—
We had learned
How to read and to write,
And we fought,
Yes, with all of our might—
We are fierce:
We're like steel; we don't pierce—

We were faithful
Through the toughest of years—
We have earned every honor and grace,
As we've come from a mighty long way—
This is true,
And my tribute to you,
You, my sisters
Of the ebony hue—

We are strength...to the furthest extent;
We are queens—
Who descended from kings.

The Poet's Commentary

I see the lady,
I see the lady I call my Nana.
I see the lady,
I see the lady I call my Mama.
I see the lady,
I see the lady I call my sister.
I see the lady,
I see the lady I call my daughter.
I see the lady,
I see the lady who is me.

I see the lady,
I see the lady who has withstood the trial and tribulation of a
ruthless generational history.

Not of her own accord has the Black woman withstood, but only by the tender mercy of the Lord has the Black woman: breathing into life the past, present, and future of the ugly, the bad, and the good,
I present to every one of you ... *This Womanhood*.

"Operation imPlantation"
Genre: Tanka

The Synopsis

This production of the written word, in the subgenre of micropoetry, intends to witness the wicked workings of Satan through those human operatives in the world that occupy its leading branches of Science and Technology.

The Poem:

They're already damned:
Those who have received the "Chip"
In their heads and hands:
Slaves to man's technology;
Doomed for all eternity.

The Poet's Commentary

IT IS A MAN'S NUMBER.

A cashless society? Do not trust it. Fear tactics? Trust them not. Lies told to disguise the truth? Believe them not. The Class Structure in Society - used as a weapon to attack one's self-esteem? Surrender not to it.

All of the above are the main components used to lead the impressionable—and perhaps even unlearned—individual astray. These have one common purpose, and that is to shove impressionable—and even unlearned—men, women, and children right over the edge into a deep valley of complete and utter self-destruction.
Microchipping, particularly of humans, is the ultimate evil. It is the most atrocious (and inhumane) technology there is, and no one should be deceived—or forced by fear tactics—into undergoing its invasive processes. No, not even one. Because of its sudden growth in worldwide popularity, I felt compelled to compose *Operation imPlantation* in rapid-fire response. And it is my sincerest hope that all of you will open your minds to sound wisdom: for it will save your life, even your eternal soul.

No one needs to penetrate your bodies with any form of invasive technology, regardless of what anyone says. One need not be paranoid, only vigilant to abstain yourselves from such a vicious raping of your bodies.

Be faithful, be at peace, and watch out for yourselves. You don't need to have a damn microchip implanted in your hand to open a door. All you need to do is grab hold of the doorknob or door handle and open it yourself. If you can't be issued a key or a keycard, you don't need it.

Do not allow anyone to lie to you and deceive you into self-destruction using "convenience" as an excuse to give in. Because that is what it will be: a lie.

Watch out for yourselves.

"Dance, Nigger, Dance"
Genre: Satirical

The Synopsis

This production of the written word, in poetic form, intends to witness the fiery wiles of spiritual warfare on those who continuously cower to subserviency and self-denigration – despite being released from a culture of oppression and societal enslavement.

Here, spiritual warfare is all in one's mind; hence, the *Conditioned Negro*.

The Poem:

Watch the nigger:

Watch the nigger as he does his jungle dance,
Before the face of the White man—

Watch the nigger:

Watch the nigger play the lesser
To his European oppressor—

Watch the nigger:

Watch the nigger disown his own
For the White man's dollar;
Watch the nigger get overthrown
In a way that makes me wanna holler—

Watch the nigger:

Watch the nigger shuck and jive
To keep the stereotypical folklore alive—

Watch the nigger:

Watch the nigger on display in his symbolic cage;
Watch the nigger as he implodes from hopelessness
In his self-destructive rage—

Watch the nigger:

Watch the nigger as he hustles to please;
Watch the nigger as he bustles to appease—

Watch the nigger:

Watch the nigger on display in his symbolic cage;
Watch the nigger as he continues to coon and buffoon,
Even in this very day and age—

Watch the nigger.

The Poet's Commentary

"My people are destroyed for lack of knowledge."
—Hosea 4:6

THE MODERN-DAY MINSTREL.

To this very day, such men refuse to leave the plantations of their minds. To this day, such men still believe that they are inferior, particularly to the ones of European descent. To this very day, such men hate not only their outward reflection but also those who share it. To this day, such men put their faith in a long-dead Massa rather than in Father God, who lives forever. To this very day, such men give away their power to others, particularly those who hate them. To this day, such men are those who, instead of building their own companies, prefer to play the sickening role of the subservient and begging fool within companies founded by others. To this very day, such men disregard the immense power of economics, electing to toss their resources into the coffers of those who blatantly hate them. To this day, such men subject themselves to much humiliation and disregard at the expense of their integrity.
To. This. Very. Day.

Indeed, such men would be willing to bullwhip themselves—to save their modern-day oppressors the trouble of having to do it for them. Indeed, such men will kick themselves in the ass—to make sure their modern-day oppressors do not have to go to the trouble of doing it for them. Like the children of Israel in the days of old are such men. For such modern men long to return to the various enslavements of their oppressors. As the men of old had been, so are they. Like the (rebellious) men of old, these also groan and grumble in the sight of God about their newfound liberation: for in this modern-day (wannabe ancient) Egypt, such men desire to be beaten into subjection and stomped down beneath the leaden feet its false Pharaohs.

This illness is what happens when one has had a conditioned mind for over four-hundred years. Rather than treating themselves to the filet mignon of life, such people seek out the scraps in life. Not because they prefer the least, but only because they keep getting told that the least is all they're worth.

All they know is the same old song and dance. And they've perfected the dance. They've perfected the dance, and Satan—operating through flesh-and-blood humans—has perfected the tune to which they dance. And as surely as the sun rises and sets, the enemy of all Mankind will continue to spin that tired-ass record until someone finally breaks it, that it should be played—and danced to—no more.

SHOW HIM YOUR FAITH, NOT YOUR WORKS.

My dearest men and women? Obedience—to God—is better than sacrifice. Learn to obey Him, and He'll make you the head, not the tail. Always remember that.

Here, the man was the focus because the man is before the woman; therefore, the man has the greater shame.

Bonus Material

"The Black Girl"
Genre: Lyric/Dramatic

The Synopsis

This production of the written word, in poetic form, is a literary adaptation of an original composition from the Cat Ellington song catalog.

The Poem/Song:

I'm a Black girl,
And I was born into this world of divisions—
To a mother who was all shuffled up
In the world system—
You know, a Black girl,
A Black girl ain't much welcome
In this hateful culture of contentions—

The system failed the Black girl
In this world—

I'm a Black girl,
And I was raised on the South Side of Chicago...
In the ghetto—
We received public aid,
And I attended a public school:
I was in the "class" of the poor—
I wore the same ol' clothes over and over,
'Cause new ones, we couldn't afford—

The system failed the Black girl In this world—
The system failed the Black girl In this world—

Black girl—
Black girl—
Black girl—

Black girl—
Black girl—
Black girl—

Just say no
To the status quo—
Just say no
To the status quo—

Black girl?
Where you at in this world?
Just say no

169

To the status quo—

Black girl?
Where you at in this world?
Just say no
To the status quo—

The Poet's Commentary

THE LEGACY OF THE BLACK GIRL.

One of my most cherished works from the Cat Ellington
song catalog is *The Black Girl*. The piece is a passionate
anthem inspired by my childhood. The poem/song comes
from my upbringing in some of the most legendary (and
historic) communities on the South Side of Chicago,
including Kenwood/Hyde Park, Washington Park, Jackson
Park, Bronzeville, and Douglas.

A proud product of the inner-city, I wrote *The Black Girl* as
a personal tribute to my life and education - as well as my
community's subjection to the city's culture of racism and
segregation.

Originally written as a basic structure (of words) in 1983, I
soon arranged a simple musical composition, and *The Black
Girl* was born as a song. Ironically, the piece was also a
mutation of poetry; hence its "crossover" into a literary
adaptation.

While I would not have done so under other circumstances, my love for my friends and mentors, Dorothy Luckett, Melvin Gaynor, and Gary Martin, helped with my decision to include *The Black Girl* on these pages.

Here's to ya!

"The Black Girl"
Words by Cat Ellington
©2019 The Black Jaguar Music Company (ASCAP)

Pardon the intrusion,
But you are now at the conclusion.

Ha!
Now that's a rhythmic fusion!

Coming November 2019

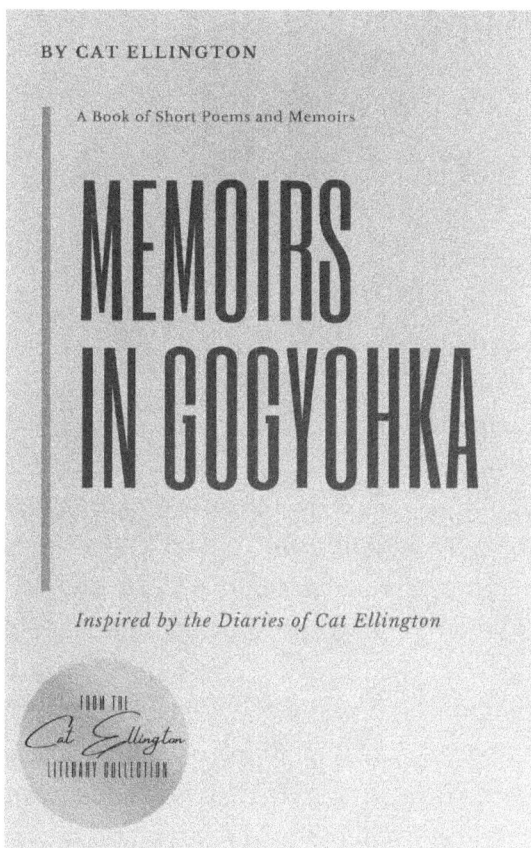

BY CAT ELLINGTON

A Book of Short Poems and Memoirs

MEMOIRS IN GOGYOHKA

Inspired by the Diaries of Cat Ellington

FROM THE
Cat Ellington
LITERARY COLLECTION

Memoirs in Gogyohka: A Book of Short Poems and
Memoirs
Imprint: Quill Pen Ink Publishing
Cover Tint: Mandarin

About the Author

Cat Ellington is an American songwriter, casting director, poet, author, and entrepreneur from Chicago, IL. She is best known for her creative contributions to the diverse industries and fields of music, movies, art, and literature.

Cat Ellington's professional credits list a collection of nonfiction books, including the Reviews by Cat Ellington series, The Making of Dual Mania, More Imaginative Than Ordinary Speech, Memoirs in Gogyohka, and You Can Quote Me On That. In film and music, Ellington's credentials include her work on the psychological thriller, "Dual Mania," and its soundtrack—on which she wrote five original songs: "The Book of Us," "I'm Still in Love," "Something in Your Eyes," "Gett Out," and "I Do."

Outside of her professional element, the award-winning creative enjoys reading, listening to music, cooking, collecting vintage and modern charm bracelets, watching movies and classic TV shows, sailing, jet-skiing, playing tennis, and eating frozen yogurt – lots of it.

Cat Ellington on Amazon: Books, Biography, Blog, Audiobooks, Kindle

Cat Ellington at the Award-Winning Boutique Domain

Cat Ellington at The Review Period with Cat Ellington

Cat Ellington at IMDb

Cat Ellington at Goodreads

www.ingramcontent.com/pod-product-compliance
Lightning Source LLC
Chambersburg PA
CBHW031958040426
42448CB00006B/412